"An easy read with very practical approaches to untangle the anxious mind. Exercises and prompts solidify the learning. A must-read for all for good mental health."

—May Kazem, *M.D.*

"Let Go of the Outcome but don't let go of this book. What a wonderfully written book. It gave me insight into both the way our minds work and the role our sensations play. Through the author's personal reflections, client stories, and exercises I found each chapter opened a door to another aspect of behaviour and awareness. I highly recommend this book to anyone looking to better understand themselves or others."

—Cookie Boyle, *Author*

"This book is one of a kind in the sense that it simplifies all the challenging concepts of psychology and makes it accessible to anyone at any level. It is beautifully and clearly written and organized. The pictures and key take-home points are all you need to make a change with a huge positive impact on your life. A privilege to read. Thank you for sharing your experience with the world Bea."

—Iren Tavakoli, *M.D.*

"This book was highly readable and easy to understand for the layman. The extensive use of diagrams and exercises clarifies points. The frequent use of photos helps keep the book fresh and makes it easy to focus on the material. I like the emphasis on the brain's ability to adapt—and the explanation about how being grateful naturally leads to more happiness, less negativity, and better self-esteem. Good work!"

—Arlene Renney, *R.N.*

"One day, while thanking Bea for sharing her knowledge and methods at a workshop she presented to our 'Joan of Arc' discussion group, Bea voiced her desire to write a book to share her knowledge of psychology with people outside her clinical setting and wished she had the time. When I offered to be her scribe our 'book mornings' began. Each week I shared her dream more.

We shared the hope that an understanding of brain function + counseling scenarios + memorable illustrations could = an understanding of the effect emotions have on our lives and how we can process them to enrich our quality of life.

Over the next year Bea's knowledge and, I like to think, some of my questions and suggestions for lay reader understanding, provided a logical sequence and presentation for you, the Reader. I'm pleased that Bea's goal has been realized and that you have this book in your hands. I wish you and your circles of influence a full life of letting things fall together."

—Louise Corrall, *B.A.*

"Dr. Mackay's new book makes the theory and practice of emotion processing very accessible for a large audience with varied needs and quests. The case studies, practical steps to follow, meaningful visuals, and paths to go further provide a holistic reading experience. Whether one opts to scan images, read from beginning to end, or focus on a particular chapter, everyone will benefit from this piece of wisdom. A fantastic and powerful tool for therapists and their clients alike."

—Hélène Morizur, *Psychologist and Artist*

"As I went from one page to another I felt like I got to know the author on a very intimate level. Dr. Bea Mackay introduces us to complex notions and then shares stories from her personal life and from her practice to illustrate everything. My favourite part of the book is that each chapter ends with practical guidance on how to help yourself and those around you."

—Konstantin Melkov, *Bookkeeper*

Let Go of the Outcome

AND LET THINGS FALL TOGETHER

Written by Bea Mackay

Edited by Tereza Racekova

Graphics by Lesley Wexler

beainbalance.com

ISBN 978-1-7386371-0-2

To my sons Colin and Angus, whom I love deeply.
They are at the core of my work, and without them,
this book would not exist.

Contents

Preface

Years ago, a doctor who referred patients to my newly started practice took me out for dinner. She explained that she often asked the referred patients how their therapy sessions went. Most of them said that it was good to talk to someone. However, in response to a session with me, she could see that the clients were already making positive changes. What puzzled me was that most of them didn't realize that the therapy was making the difference.

I was delighted to hear this and took her feedback seriously, as this was the first indication that I was doing something different from other psychologists. At the time, I didn't know what I was doing or how I was doing it to have such a therapeutic impact. So I started to pay attention.

Good News! I have figured it out! It has taken me many years, and I finally can share what I do that makes my work with clients effective.

My work with clients comes from my training in Gestalt and Adlerian therapy. Gestalt therapy focuses on the sensations, while Adlerian therapy focuses on the structure and development of human beings. In Gestalt therapy, I learned to focus on the sensations being experienced. From Adlerian therapy, I learned about how human beings develop a modus operandi as they mature. In working with clients, I learned that when I help them stay in the moment and facilitate their expression of feelings to the depths, they exhibit more practical and intuitive behaviours.

It took some time to realize why this worked; that the function of the breath (breathing deeply) allows the brain to create new neural pathways, transcending our old ways of thinking and feeling and experiencing new sensations.

Emotions and feelings are all about the quality of sensations we experience, varying from unpleasant to pleasant and intense to calm. Actions and behaviours are influenced by the quality of sensations we experience. Some sensations we embrace more of, and some we avoid.

In this book, I share this knowledge and my experiences with the hope that my readers will also gain knowledge and help.

Read a Little at a Time

1. Open the book 30 minutes before you go to sleep and look at one or two layouts.

2. Close the book and go to sleep.

3. Let your brain do its magic—synthesize and make sense out of it.

Acknowledgements

This book has been a long time in the making, and many people have contributed to its creation.

I want to thank Dr. Teresa Cordoni, who, early in my career, alerted me to the fact that I am helping people make significant changes in their lives and that I am doing it differently from most counsellors and therapists.

I want to thank Gary Mahler, whose presence and wise words allowed me to dream again, which resulted in writing this book.

I want to thank Louise Corrall, my good friend and cheer-leader, who helped me get the words out of my head and onto paper.

I want to thank Amanda Johnson, who helped me put the first draft together.

I want to thank my publishing team, who I am incredibly proud of and who made this book possible. We worked so well together, each providing our expertise. It was so much fun!

I want to thank Tereza Racekova, my amazing editor, who took my material and made it flow like magic.

I want to thank Lesley Wexler, my incredible graphic artist, who created the brilliant cover, images, diagrams, and pictures.

Lastly, I want to thank all my clients for trusting me with their cares and concerns.

Bea Team

Introduction

Personal Story—I'm Having a Panic Attack!

I woke up in abject terror. It was 5:00 a.m., and the hotel room was dark. Today was the day; I was presenting my first workshop at an international level. I was terrified. I felt as though I was going to die.

I knew my level of terror was unnecessary, given my circumstances. It was only a one-hour workshop of basic material. Logically and rationally, I knew I was scaring myself. I knew I was overreacting. However, that did not stop the *sensations* of cold white terror coursing through my body from the top of my head to the bottom of my feet.

Thankfully, I knew what I had to do. I needed to *process* the terror. So, I lay in bed and breathed through the sensations of terror. The hotel room was my container for *processing*. I knew I would not be disturbed. For two hours, I lay there, sensing and breathing through the waves of terror—letting go of the outcome. I stopped trying to feel okay by reasoning with myself or figuring out why I was feeling the way I was feeling. I accepted that I was terrified, but I stayed with the sensations of fear and breathed through them. By 7:00 a.m., the waves of terror had stopped. I was tired but felt calm. Something in my head had shifted, but I did not know what at the time.

I got ready and went to present my workshop. It went okay; nothing great, nothing bad.

Since then, I have been able to present at workshops easily and with a normal level of excitement.

I grew up in the '40s and '50s. I was the youngest daughter of farmers. Both my parents quit school at the end of Grade

7 because my father, the eldest of ten children, had to help his father run the family farm, and my mother's father, also a farmer, saw no use educating a girl who was going to become a farmer's wife.

Fortunately for me, my parents valued education, especially my mother, because she had wanted to become a geriatric nurse. She often said to me, "Get an education so that you won't have to work as hard as your father and me."

My parents were not sophisticated people. They did not know how to be diplomatic. They went through the depression of the '30s. For them, life was serious business.

Parenting in that era was tough: "Spare the rod and spoil the child." There was corporal punishment in schools. At home, my parents would strap us. I remember the harsh voice of my father when he would say, "If you're going to cry, I'll give you something to cry about." I also remember the harsh voice of my mother, who would ask, "Do you want me to get the strap?" When my parents spoke, I got scared, held my breath, and shut my eyes to stop the tears from flowing. I certainly did not learn to *process* my emotions growing up. In fact, I learned the opposite. I learned to hide any emotions as best as possible because it was dangerous to show what I felt.

We are all shaped by our early experiences. I believe the sensations of satisfaction I had when I made sense of what was going on in my life as a child led me to a lifetime of wanting to know and understand people and the world around me. Understanding made life so much easier. It has also led me to want to educate others to understand themselves and the world around them.

I want to give people something to do differently; I want them to know that they can handle the discomfort of emotion with new behaviours. Once they can tolerate the sensations, they will no longer be afraid to feel them. They will behave naturally, knowing to breathe through any uncomfortable sensations as or when they come along.

"*Newborn babies come into a complicated world in a very vulnerable state. They have an innate ability to process their emotions. As time goes on, the developing brain constantly adapts and adjusts to the environment and creates neural pathways for every experience. My goal with Let Go of the Outcome and Let Things Fall Together is to offer a comprehensive guide that examines and provides tools to help people emotionally thrive.*"

—Bea Mackay

CHAPTER ONE

Know Your Mind, Know Yourself

"Lose your mind and come to your senses." —Fritz Perls

Once living organisms come into existence, they strive to survive. Mother Nature wants each species to survive, so she programmed their DNA to help them succeed. The strong survive, and the weak die off. Many come into existence; some survive to procreate and pass on their genes. We arrived on this planet through no choice of our own. We did not decide to come into existence, but since we exist, we have an innate drive to survive, cope, and thrive.

SURVIVING: Food, clothing, attachment, shelter, sleep, connection, and safety. A lot of our thinking and feeling is geared toward survival. Survival is instinctive.

COPING: Lack of food, clothing, shelter, and dealing with difficult people, poor conditions, poor health, and lack of safety.

THRIVING: Living well, developing fully into all we can be intellectually, physically, and emotionally. We experience "flow," so we are creative, spontaneous, and productive. Our basic needs are met (food, clothing, shelter), and we have a support system in place, such as family and community, and are protected by and connected to others.

Newborn babies come into a complicated world in a very vulnerable state. From the moment they are conceived, they adapt to their environment in utero and after birth. In the first year, their brains grow the fastest; in the second year, the second-fastest; and in the third year, the third-fastest. After that, their brain growth begins to slow down yet keeps growing until their mid-twenties. While the formation of neural pathways slows down, the brain continually adapts until death.

The developing brain is constantly adapting and adjusting to the environment—geographically, culturally, and socio-economically—and the current circumstances to which we are born (war/peace; feast/famine; quality of family/home; quality of mothering/care-taking). The brain develops neural pathways for every experience. In our early years, the brain creates neural pathways at an astonishing speed.

We are all shaped by the quality of life's conditions, circumstances, and the people who raise us, teach us, and interact with us. We are all shaped and influenced by our early experiences.

How do we know we exist? We know because we have receptors in our brains and bodies that pick up data through our senses—smell, sight, hearing, taste, and touch. These receptors gather data from the universe, detect or sense information through various ways, and convey it to the brain. There are also proprioceptors in our muscles that inform our brain where our body parts are so that we can coordinate them. According to Scottish genealogist Bruce Durie,[1] humans have many more senses, at least twenty-one, meaning we have more senses than we thought.

Receptors bring all this sensory data to our brains so that our brains can create meaning. Why? So that we can survive. Survival is key to the evolution of the brain.

---

1 Article: Why you have at least 21 senses. NEW SCIENTIST Issue: 2484 January 2005.

Instinctive Survival Behaviours

On Earth, no matter what the species, basic methods of survival have become instinctual, that is, built into the DNA over thousands of years. The survival behaviours of Fight, Flight, and Freeze have developed over millions of years. The organisms that survived passed on their genes to the next generation, and so on.

These behaviours are so ingrained in our DNA that people's bodies and minds behave as though their fears are life-threatening.

Fawning

As I've said previously, I had a mother who would blow up and strap us kids. I would try not to let her see what was happening inside of me, what I was thinking, and what I was feeling because it could be dangerous. The consequences were harsh; she might blow up at me, which is scary, and strap me, which was terrifying.

My father was more placid and calm, I knew he adored me and I felt adored by him. Because my mother never blew up when he was present, I felt safe with him. Although he did not like my tears and would say to me gruffly, "If you're going to cry, I'll give you something to cry for", he never hit me. Or blew up at me.

Personal Story—Fawning Through Seduction

My ex-husband was somewhat like my mother, controlling and unsafe, and somewhat like my father, loving and safe. When he got angry, I would hide my fright and often was able to seduce him out of it.

But I did not know I was doing that at the time. When we were in conflict, I would get sensations of fear (intense and unpleasant). I learned through trial and error to use seduction to end it; then, the sensations for both for us would shift. The unpleasant sensations would go away, and the pleasant sensations would be there for both of us.

Little did I know what I was doing. I did not realize that I was actually feeding a negative interactive dynamic between the two of us. I just knew that when he got angry, I got unpleasant/intense sensations, which went away when I could seduce him.

I was trying to make the relationship work.

Because our love language was the same—touch—(sex, lovemaking, cuddling, kissing) was how we connected in a safe/bonding way.

It worked for a long time (29 years), and then it didn't.

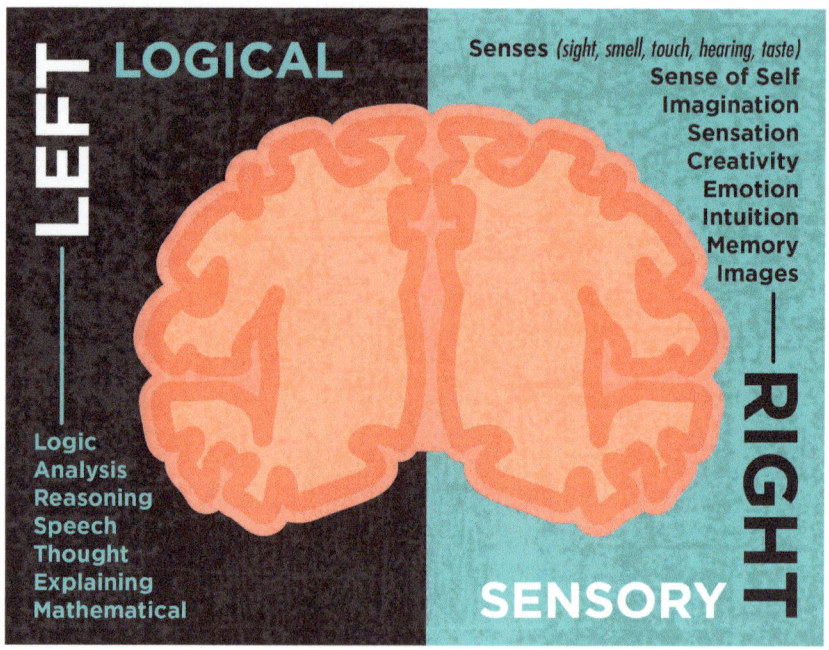

Human beings have been evolving for millions of years. To best understand how our minds and emotions function, let's look at the brain and its parts and how they work separately and together.

Human beings evolved separately from animals sometime around five to ten million years ago[2] because the neocortex (the part of the brain that makes us human and differentiates us from animals) began to evolve and grow markedly larger.

At this time, the cavemen needed to leave the cave in search of food and materials. Therefore, because of their different roles, men's and women's brains developed somewhat differently.

Two Hemispheres of the Brain

The brain has two hemispheres that co-exist side-by-side.[2] Each can function separately from the other, giving us two types of intelligence.

The Logical Brain

The Logical Brain is responsible for speech, understanding language, thought, mathematical and analytical reasoning, and aspects of our consciousness. The unique facet of the Logical Brain is that there is no feeling or sensation in any part of it. It does not register fatigue, hunger, pain, sickness, or emotion. This hemisphere thinks very rapidly—thousands of thoughts per day.

Because the Logical Brain does not feel, people can survive situations in which they are injured/terrified. They can get themselves or others out of danger, stay hidden until the danger passes, or withstand hunger for long periods.

---

[2] Joseph, R. Neuropsychiatry, Neuropsychology, and Clinical Neuroscience: Emotion Evolution, Cognition, Language, Memory, Brain Damage, and Abnormal Behaviour. 2nd ED. Williams & Wilkins. Baltimore, Maryland, USA, 1996

The Sensory Brain

The Sensory Brain is responsible for picking up all the non-verbal data around us, including the environment, our sense of self, our sense of others, and making sense of all the aspects of emotionality.

To be human is to be in a state of consciousness that enables one to think about one's own existence and experience and analyze the universe and all that is in it. Thought occurs in the Logical Brain, which has the capacity for language. Meanwhile, the Sensory Brain detects and registers all the sensory data with nerve endings designed/evolved to receive light, sound, touch, smell, taste, extra-sensory, and other data from the universe.

The Logical Brain helped the cavemen survive. The cavemen needed to survive so that they could provide for the women and their clan. If they did not survive in the wild, their clan would die. The men who got sick, tired, emotional, or did not have the stamina to keep going, did not survive. The men who could stay in the Logical Brain were more likely to survive and return to the clan. If they were tired, they did not feel tired. If they were injured, they did not feel pain. If they were terrified, they did not feel fear. If they were sick, they did not feel the symptoms. Because they stayed in their Logical Brain, they managed to keep going and get back to the clan. The cavemen who returned to the clan passed their genes onto their offspring, making the next generations stronger.

Meanwhile, the women stayed at the caves and multi-tasked while the men were away. They cooked, skinned the animals, collected firewood, tended to the children, cleaned the home, and nurtured relationships. If they felt sick, they could lie down; if they were tired, they could rest; if they were hurt, they would feel pain. There were times when the women needed to block out sensations and operate from thinking. This included times when they needed to haul water long distances, when animals stalked them, or when

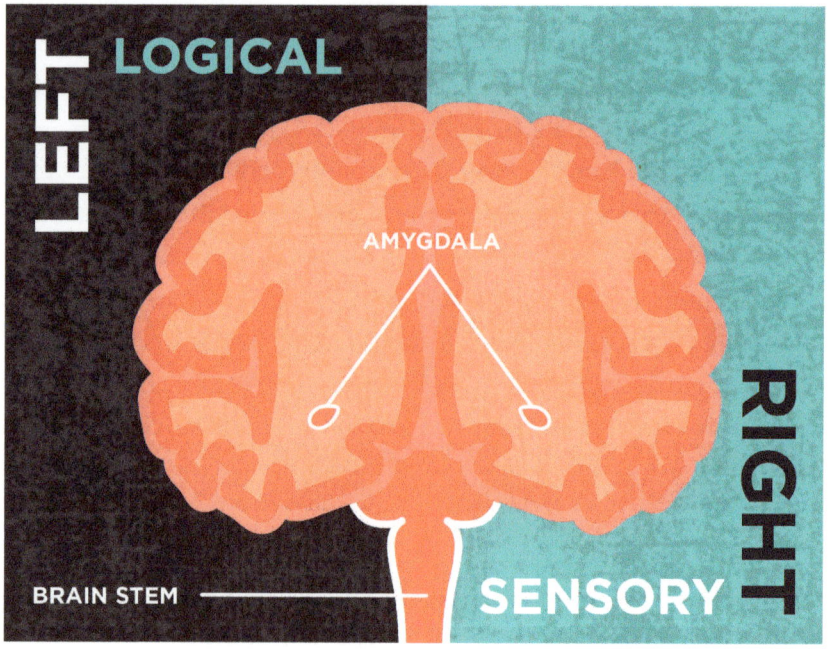

their shelter was threatened. However, this did not often happen, at least not for extended periods.[3]

Today, we have more information on how the brain is structured and its functions than ever before. Magnetic Resonance Imaging (MRI) has allowed scientific research to be conducted on the brain, which is the most complicated organ in our bodies.

The Brain Stem

The brain stem, which is rarely talked about, keeps the body functioning. The brain stem supports the organism's basic functions. Many brain stem functions, such as walking, chewing, and breathing, are performed reflexively, which does not require thinking or planning.[4]

The Amygdala—The Overseer

An important part of the brain is the amygdala. There are two amygdalae, one in each brain hemisphere, about the size of an almond, and they play a significant role in the brain's functioning.

---

[3] Joseph, R. Neuropsychiatry, Neuropsychology, and Clinical Neuroscience: Emotion Evolution, Cognition, Language, Memory, Brain Damage, and Abnormal Behaviour. 2nd ED. Williams & Wilkins. Baltimore, Maryland, USA, 1996.
[4] Joseph, R. Neuropsychiatry, Neuropsychology, and Clinical Neuroscience: Emotion Evolution, Cognition, Language, Memory, Brain Damage, and Abnormal Behaviour. 2nd ED. Williams & Wilkins. Baltimore, Maryland, USA, 1996

The amygdala is like the wheelhouse of a supertanker. Every part of a supertanker, above and below water, is connected to the wheelhouse. The wires, mechanisms, computers, and devices are needed to convey immense amounts of information to the central place on the ship. From the wheelhouse, the captain can control the whole ship.

If there is any danger, such as a fire, leak, breakdown, or other problem, the wheelhouse can detect it and attend to it immediately. The wheelhouse is always on alert for danger within the ship and beyond it.

The amygdala has the capacity and ability to constantly monitor the data coming in from the other parts of our body, including the senses, other parts of the brain, and the environment. It is on alert for internal and external danger.

In the time of the cavemen, the amygdala alerted the adrenal glands to pump adrenaline into the bloodstream when there was danger. The danger the cavemen experienced was often life-threatening, so the adrenaline fueled their muscles for the actions of Fight, Flight, or Freeze.

Today, humans still experience the Fight, Flight, and Freeze reactions. However, in many situations, the danger we experience is not life-threatening, yet the brain reacts and responds as though it is, i.e., losing one's job, failing an exam, losing a lover, or dealing with an abusive parent, spouse, boss, etc.

When children grow up in dangerous situations, experience difficult circumstances, or live in families that are not safe, their amygdalae are so used to being on alert and therefore so used to sending signals to the adrenal glands to pump adrenaline into the bloodstream that it is difficult for them to enjoy happy, carefree, and fun activities for any length of time. They develop many neural pathways for vigilance and danger. For them, life is

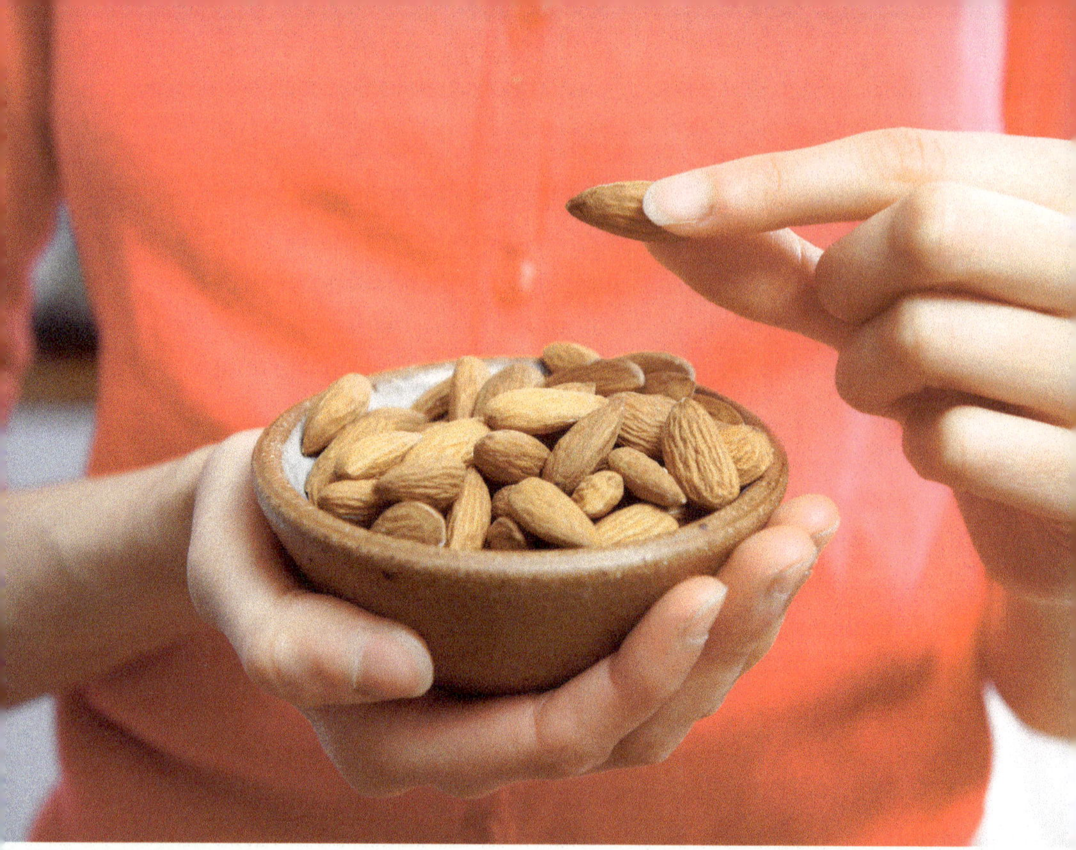
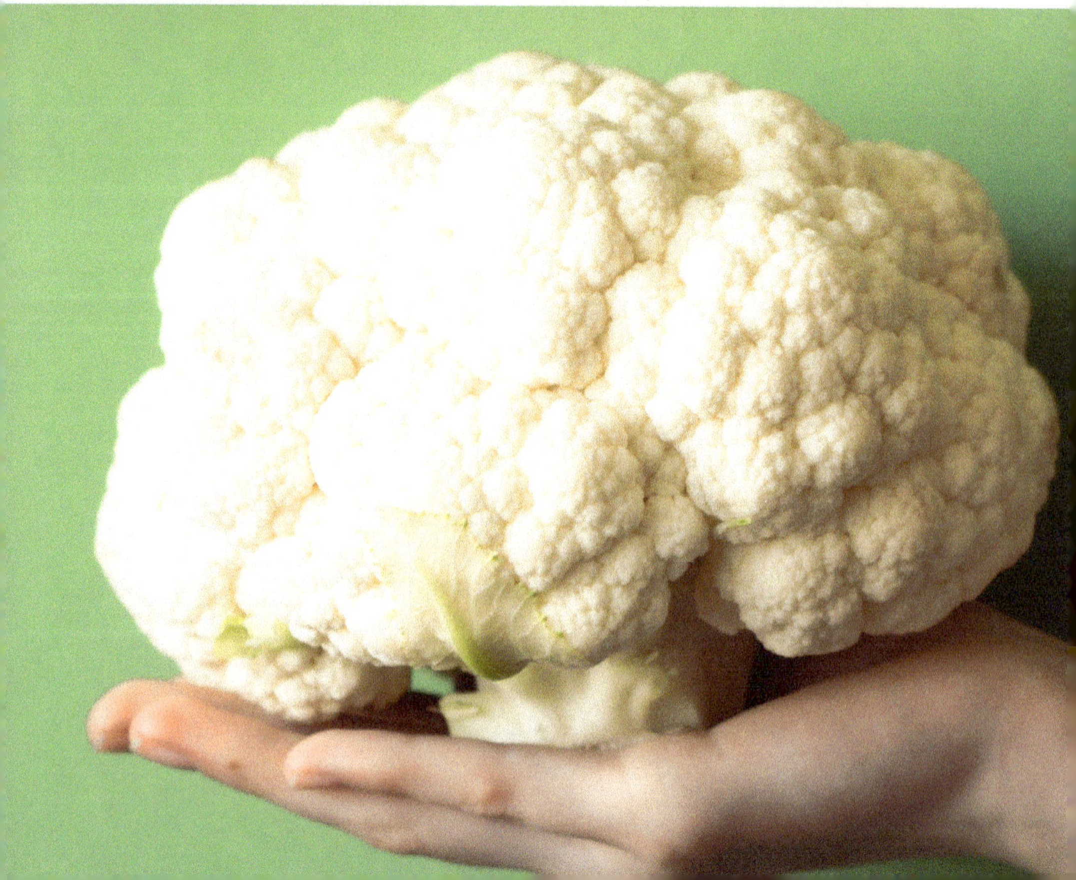

serious business. They are on alert. If they let their guard down, they often experience serious consequences. They usually suffer from nightmares and symptoms such as anxiety, numbness, and bed-wetting. They have some neural pathways for play and fun, but not many. As adults, it is difficult for them to relax and feel calm. It is like a hot water tap that cannot be fully turned off.

Children who grow up in mostly happy, safe, loving families develop many neural pathways for living well. They will naturally *process* emotions as allowed and modelled by supportive parents, other family members, and communities. This is what every child should be able to do growing up. This is what is natural and psychologically healthy.

The amygdala is also important in emotional and motivational functioning. It serves as the seat of social and emotional intelligence.[5] It is responsible for generating and maintaining mood. The amygdala also plays a role in sexual activity and sex drive. For its size, the amygdala has an immense role in human functioning, and its most crucial role is to coordinate the two brain hemispheres.

The brain can get overwhelmed by too much data. However, generally speaking, the more data we have, the more we make sense of our current situations, and better decisions precipitate. By making better decisions, we are likely to survive, cope, and thrive. While the Logical Brain makes decisions, our decisions are informed by the experiences that stem from the Sensory Brain. Therefore, it is crucial to use both. This means we need to connect more with our Sensory Brain by getting in touch with our emotions, feelings, and sensations.

---

[5] Joseph, R. Neuropsychiatry, Neuropsychology, and Clinical Neuroscience: Emotion Evolution, Cognition, Language, Memory, Brain Damage, and Abnormal Behaviour. 2nd ED. Williams & Wilkins. Baltimore, Maryland, USA, 1996

Understanding the Brains—Logical Brain and Sensory Brain

People are strongly motivated to understand why and how they came to feel what they feel. Often, it helps to understand this, and it may even evoke positive change. However, understanding alone does not induce change because people do not know what else to do; they often get stuck in the Logical Brain re-analyzing and re-thinking with the hope/intent to get the change they seek. What they do not know is that understanding is *not necessary* for change.

The answer is to shift from thinking to sensing—to shift out of the Logical Brain by interrupting the thinking and focusing on the sensations in the body. Typically, people do not want to feel painful emotions because they are afraid of the *sensations* as they are intense and unpleasant.

KEY*

|■| Fear/Insecurity

⟨⟩ Disgust/Repulsion

〜〜 Sadness/Remorse

↻ Slight Shame/Humiliation/
Embarrassment

*More information about
emotional sensations on
page 62

Understanding is Not Necessary for Change

AJ, a man in his early 30s, had had many girlfriends but couldn't seem to get past six months with any of them before he broke off the relationship. He always feared the woman would eventually reject him, so he would reject her before she could reject him.

He had become tired of constantly starting over. He was ready for a permanent relationship, so he came for therapy.

Halfway through our second session, he said to me, "I don't know why I'm so afraid of rejection."

"I know why. Would you like me to tell you?" I said.

"Yes," responded AJ.

"From everything you've told me, I understand that your mother went back to work when you were one year old and that until you were five, your beloved grandmother adored you and spent a lot of time with you. When your twin sisters were born, she turned her attention to them, and you were devastated. Since then, you've been worried that it will happen again. At school, you said that in Grade 2, the teacher focused a lot of her attention on you, but when a new boy arrived in class, her attention went to him. Again, you were hurt and felt rejected. You began to imagine and fear that there was something wrong with you. That's why you fear rejection. Would you say that was accurate?

"Yes, that's right," AJ responded.

"Does knowing that change anything?"

"No," AJ admitted.

"Exactly, you can know all the logic and reasoning about what you feel, but it often does not change anything. It no longer matters why you are afraid of rejection. What matters is that you are afraid of feeling rejected, and you are trying everything you can to avoid experiencing the intense unpleasant sensations again. You need to get out of your Logical Brain and into your Sensory Brain."

I'm Okay as Long as I'm Busy

My client, Inez, was a very experienced and successful commercial real estate agent. She had been sexually abused by her father from a young age and had never had any treatment. Instead, she had coped with it by developing a lifestyle that required her to stay in her Logical Brain. By staying in her Logical Brain, she could block out the memories and sensations of the abuse. She could never rest.

Inez had an extremely busy career as a real estate agent, which kept her occupied seven days per week. She was very good at what she did. When she took holidays, she travelled to different parts of the world. She scuba-dived on the Great Barrier Reef, zipped-lined in Costa Rica, cycled through the wine counties in France, hiked Machu Picchu in Peru, etc. She lived an exciting life, always busy and active, and this was how she kept her "demons" (the unhealed trauma from her childhood) in check. As long as she was busy, she didn't think of the past and didn't feel the sensations that constitute a significant part of unhealed trauma.

On some level, she was emotionally and physically exhausted by her lifestyle and realized she needed to deal with the unhealed trauma. That's when she sought therapy.

Exercise

Let's get you out of your Logical Brain and into your Sensory Brain. Some people find it difficult to get into the Sensory Brain and notice the sensations in their bodies.

Let's start with the clothes on your body:

- How do you know that you are not naked?

- You know because you feel the sensations of the clothes on your body.

Now, let's focus on your feet:

- Do one foot at a time.

- Is your (left) foot bare, or are you wearing a sock?

- If it is, feel/sense the bareness.

- If you are wearing a sock, feel the sock on your foot. See if you can feel where the top of your sock stops and your leg begins. If your leg is bare, feel the bareness.

Now, shift to the other foot:

- Is your (right) foot bare, or are you wearing a sock?

- If it is, feel/sense the bareness.

- If you are wearing a sock, feel the sock on your foot. See if you can feel where the top of your sock stops and your bare skin begins. If your leg is bare, feel the bareness.

Continue doing this by going up your entire body until you reach the top of your head:

- Now, you are more aware of your body.

How to Help Others Help Themselves

Help people articulate their experience as specifically as possible:

- Listen for the person's view and *experience* of the facts, situation, circumstances, etc. Do *not* get caught up in the content.

- Keep your advice to yourself. People may say they want advice, but they don't because either they have already tried it or considered what you are suggesting and have rejected it, or they do not want to be told what to do.

- Be a sounding board. Reflect their views and experiences to them. Help people articulate what they are thinking and feeling. Often, that is all that is needed (i.e., Do not judge; do not argue; do not reason; also, this is not the time to play the Devil's Advocate).

Key Takeaways:

- **Logical Brain = speech, understanding language, thought, mathematical and analytical reasoning, and aspects of our consciousness.**

- **Sensory Brain = non-verbal data around us, including the environment, our sense of self, our sense of others, and making sense of all the aspects of emotionality.**

CHAPTER TWO

Feel Fully,
Feel More Alive

"Therefore let your soul exalt your reason to the height of passion, that it may sing; And let it direct your passion with reason, that your passion live through its own daily resurrection, and like the Phoenix rise above its own ashes." —Kalil Gibran

LOGICAL BRAIN	SENSORY BRAIN
THINK = LEFT	FEEL = RIGHT
LOGIC = LEFT	SENSE = RIGHT
= I think I'm lonely	= I feel lonely, I'm lonely
= Analysis of feelings	= Expression of feelings
= Makes decisions	= Decisions precipitate

The Logical Brain and the Sensory Brain each have their unique functions, and both are amazing at what they can do. They can work separately, and they can work together. When they work together, they create a third function, referred to here as synthesis and integration.

The Logical Brain and the Sensory Brain help us make the healthiest sense of our lives, which precipitates actions/behaviours that best fit our current circumstances.

The Sensory Brain, the limbic system, and the body create the emotions that human beings experience, while the Logical Brain analyzes the emotions.

LOGICAL BRAIN + **SENSORY BRAIN** = **SYNTHESIS** Integration of Facts & Sensations/Feelings

For example, as hydrogen and oxygen synthesize, water is precipitated; the same is true of different brain functions. As the Logical Brain data comes together with the Sensory Brain data, it creates (precipitates) new neural pathways with new/different sensations.

$$2H + 1O = H_2O$$

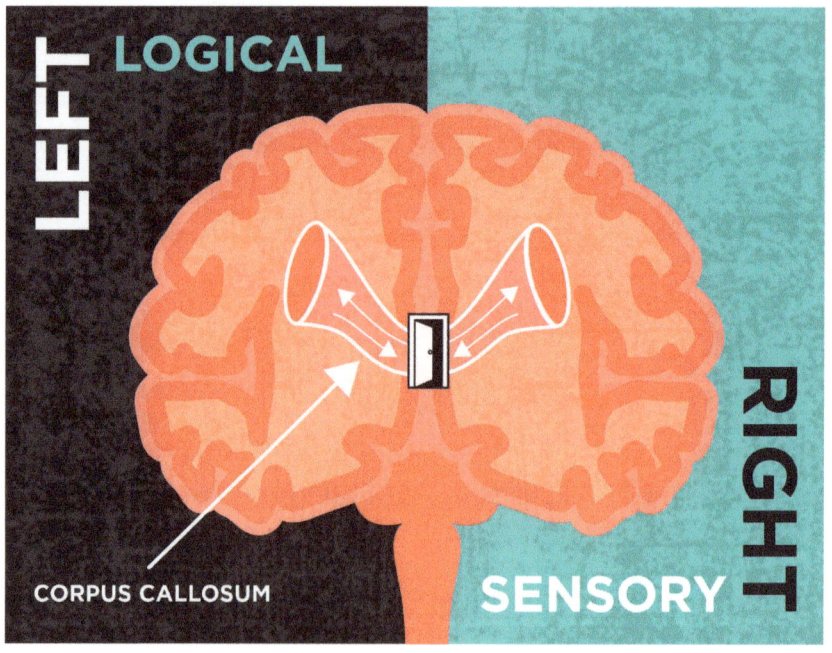

The Corpus Callosum—Connecting the Logical Brain and the Sensory Brain

The corpus callosum is a band of neurons that connect the Logical Brain and the Sensory Brain. The band of neurons is thinner in men compared to women. As mentioned in Chapter One, the male and female brains developed differently based on the different tasks required for each sex's survival. To survive, cavemen needed to stay in the Logical Brain more often, while cavewomen could freely go back and forth between the Logical Brain and the Sensory Brain.

Another factor that shaped the human brain is the influence of culture. For centuries, society has discouraged men from displaying or expressing emotions other than anger. Most men usually get angry when they need to cry because it is socially acceptable for them to be angry and NOT socially acceptable for them to cry.

On the other hand, most women usually cry when they need to be angry because it is socially acceptable for them to cry and NOT socially acceptable for them to get angry.

It is my belief that cultural pressures shaped the male and female brains.

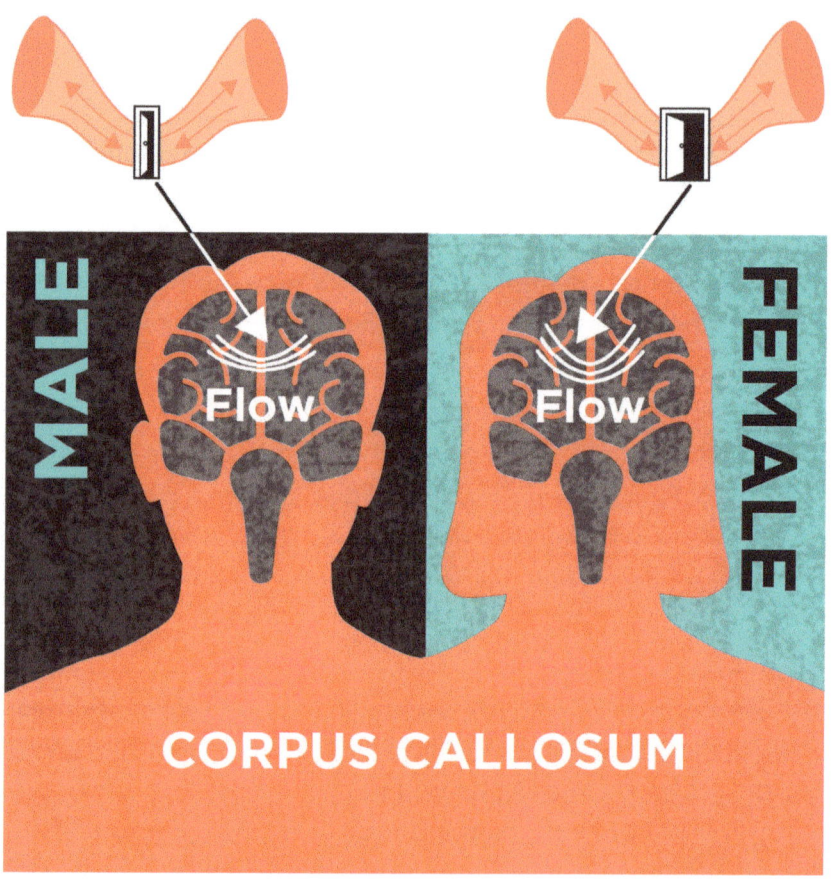

The metaphor of the doorway is used to convey the function of the corpus callosum. The corpus callosum is like a tunnel with a doorway that can be opened and closed, depending on the circumstances. The function is the same for both sexes, but for men, the doorway is narrow and more often closed, while for women, it is wider and more often open. Therefore, it is easier for men to close it and manage their emotions/sensations.[1]

When flow through the corpus callosum is blocked, the Logical Brain and Sensory Brain data cannot connect (synthesize); thus, new neural pathways cannot be formed. This can be helpful in many situations in the short term.

For example, breaking one's leg in a car accident and blocking the pain and trauma out (staying in the Logical Brain), but *managing* to get out of the car and walking to get help.

When the corpus callosum is open, it allows data flow to occur between the Logical Brain and the Sensory Brain. As the data comes together, it is synthesized, creating new neural pathways; thus, creating new perceptions, sensations, and experiences, which ultimately foster intellectual and emotional growth.

For example, after *managing* to get out of the car and walking to get help, the injured person eventually feels the sensations of pain of their broken leg and the trauma of the accident (reconnecting with the Sensory Brain) and can no longer walk on their injured leg.

---

1 Ari Berkowitz, Presidential Professor of Biology, Director of Cellular & Behavioral Neurobiology Program, University of Oklahoma— Scientists haven't found any major differences between women's and men's brains. Big Think, August 13, 2020

The Difference Between *Processing* Emotions and *Managing* Emotions

Processing Emotions:

One notices unpleasant sensations in the body.

One stays focused on the unpleasant sensations in the body.

One takes deep breaths.

One does NOT try to figure out "Why?"

One stays relaxed, breathes slowly.

One's sensations shift and change/often come in waves.

One stays calm and stays focused on sensations.

One's sensations shift and change/become less intense.

One stays calm and focuses on sensations.

One breathes through this awareness.

One's unpleasant sensations have disappeared and are completely gone.

One's new sensations come into awareness.

Even intense/pleasant sensations (of emotions) need to be processed.

Personal Story—Love Can Be Scary

One time when my son Colin was a tiny infant, asleep in his bassinette, I tiptoed into the room to peek at him. As I leaned over the bassinette, a wave of love (sensations) starting in my lower stomach, rose to fill my chest with such intensity that it scared me. For a moment, it took my breath away. I didn't know the sensations of a mother's love could be so strong.

Managing Emotions:

One notices unpleasant sensations in the body.

One shifts to the Logical Brain and asks "Why?"

One holds breath and/or breathes shallow.

One keeps trying to figure out "Why?"

One gets tense, muscles tighten.

One's unpleasant sensations increase.

One worries about physical and mental health.

One's sensations increase in intensity and unpleasantness.

One gets more worried.

One focuses on a task to deflect from/block sensations.

One forgets about sensations.

One's sensations and worries leave awareness.

People who grow up in loving, safe, and emotionally intimate family environments can receive praise, compliments, help, kindness, and reciprocate. Those who grew up in emotionally unhealthy families are uncomfortable with the sensations created from pleasant interactions because they are not used to them. They tend to push them away even though they want them.

sensations come in waves

breathe
through the waves

breathe
through the sensations

Growing up, we learn to *manage* our physical sensations. We eat when we feel the sensations of hunger, drink when we feel the sensations of thirst, sleep when we feel the sensations of fatigue, etc. Often, we need to wait to set a time to do these familiar behaviours, but these needs must eventually be met.

The same is true of our emotions. They come from living life. We learn to express them at times that are natural and appropriate. Sometimes, we need to wait to express and *process* them when it is safe and appropriate.

The Physiology of Breathing

The breath is the key to the flow of data through the corpus callosum. Holding the breath and breathing shallow blocks the flow, while deeply breathing facilitates the flow.

The diaphragm is a muscle that divides the upper body from the lower body. When the diaphragm contracts, it creates space in the upper body, and our lungs draw in air. When the diaphragm relaxes, the air is pushed out. This happens continuously without us having to think about it.

When something happens that we perceive to be dangerous or intense, positive or negative, we tend to hold our breath and/or breathe shallow. By doing so, we block the transmission of logical and sensory data through the corpus callosum.

Jumping up and down from excitement and happiness helps to *process* positive sensations because breathing is increased during this vigorous activity. With painful and difficult sensations, such as grief and loss, people tend to curl up, choke off sobs, and be less active, which blocks the *processing* of sensations.

The sensations of feelings that are not *processed* build up over time, hijacking our personal energy. Part of this personal energy is used to block/hold back the natural energy we possess, which flows and just "is."

Consider that human emotion is like a creek that is constantly flowing. If left alone, the water naturally flows. Sometimes, it overflows, and other times, it is almost dry. Then, a dam is built to hold back the natural flow of water. As the water level begins to rise, it puts more pressure on the dam. The water is now *managed*. However, if enough water is not allowed to flow, the water gets higher, and the pressure against the dam is now stronger. Therefore, the dam must be built higher and stronger to hold back the rising water, which requires more energy from the builders. Ultimately, the dam cannot be built any higher, and the water begins to spill over the top.

The water is the person's natural energy in the emotional form. If the emotion is not allowed to flow, the emotion will build up. It takes personal energy to block or stop the flow of emotion. Now, the person's energy is split—there is the natural flow of the emotions that needs *processing*, and there is the blocking of the *processing*. This leads to inner conflict and impacts one's relationship with one's self. The organism's natural emotional energy presses against the psychic structure created to block the flow. Over time, more and more of a person's energy is needed to *manage* the emotions. This means the person has less and less energy available to live life.

STACK
of
COINS

Lost Keys ———————●

Missed the Bus ——————●

Didn't Get the
Promotion ●

Splashed by a Car ———————●

She Doesn't Feel
the Same Way
About Me ——————●

Phone Broke ———————●

Eventually, something will give. The person will either live a limited life or have an emotional breakdown; they will either implode or explode. The part of the person that blocks the emotion will start to crumble and even collapse entirely, or the emotion will begin to spill over, and emotional expression will be in excess of what the situation requires—such as crying at work or outbursts of anger over small incidents, such as spilt milk. This leads to emotional exhaustion and an inability to function, which is often what a mid-life crisis involves. A person's way of operating in the world developed over time no longer works, but they do not yet have a new way of being; therefore, they stay the same. They use so much energy to *manage* their emotions that there is not enough energy to function in daily life. By breathing through the waves of sensations their personal energy will realign and all flow in the same direction.

The
CYCLE

EXPLOSION
(Outward)

PEACE | TENSION BUILDS | FATIGUE | STRESS | UNPLEASANT THOUGHTS | BODY SENSATIONS | RED FLAG

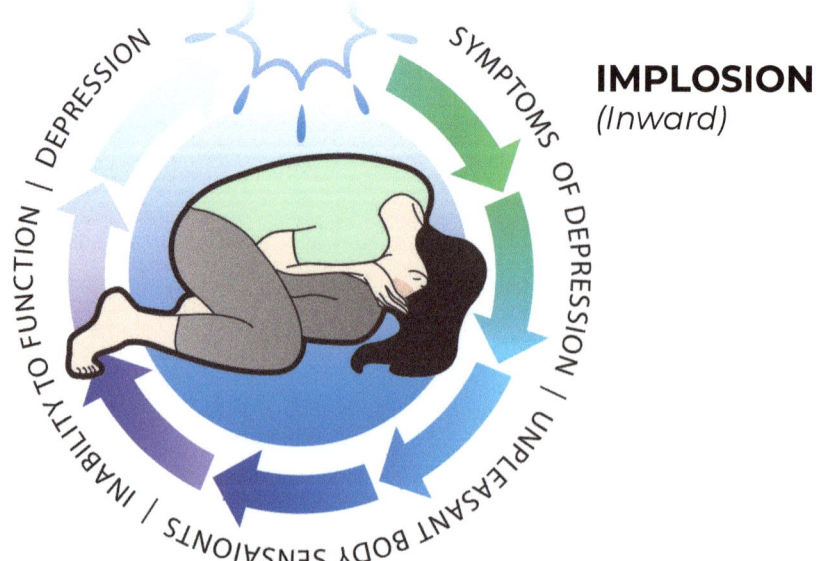

IMPLOSION
(Inward)

SYMPTOMS OF DEPRESSION | UNPLEASANT BODY SENSAIONTS | INABILITY TO FUNCTION | DEPRESSION

Built into every dam are sluice gates to regulate and control the flow of water. If there is too much water, the sluice gates are opened, and more water can flow through. This alleviates pressure on the dam so that it can hold strong. In this sense, a person can find the sluice gates in their own dam and begin to open them up by breathing while focusing on the sensations as the emotions flow through. Before the water spills over, a person can open the sluice gates and let some water (emotions) through, meaning they can begin to *process* their emotions; by creating new neural pathways they develop a new way of being.

"I cried and cried and, cried and I didn't sleep that night. And the next morning, when I woke up, I felt a tremendous shift. I'd done something, said what I felt. Still the old jealousy and anger swilling around, but it wasn't so deathly as before." —Princess Diana

An Example of Emotion Being *Processed* (*Not Managed*)

In her book, *Diana: In Her Own Words*, she talks openly about her emotions.

After seven years, Diana is fed up with trying to win her husband's affections back from his mistress, Camilla. She decides to confront Camilla.

Although terrified, she bolsters her courage and is determined to do it. She picks an occasion when there is a gathering to which she is not invited and shows up. She finds Camilla and demands that Camilla leave her husband alone. Having achieved her goal, she leaves.

She describes the emotional ride back to Buckingham Palace. Once she had confronted Camilla and was in the car, she let go and cried to the depths.

By sobbing deeply, Diana breathed through the intensely unpleasant waves of sensations. Her brain created new neural pathways that changed the quality of the sensations, transcending her old experience. From this process, she gained a new perception of herself and her circumstances. This changed her behaviours going forward.

WHAT IS, IS.

Sometimes, during this shift, the biggest temptation is to avoid feeling the sensations (a twinge, some nausea, a slight headache, etc.) and immediately shift back into the Logical Brain and figure out *why* they are feeling this way. However, it does not matter why! It also does not matter who, what, when, where, or how. What matters is that they are having these sensations and need to stay with them. What is, is. When we stay with the sensations and breathe into them, we are *processing* them; we are creating new neural pathways that precipitate new sensations, and, therefore, we evolve emotionally and change in a healthy and productive way. As we reconnect with our bodies, we feel more connected to ourselves.

I'm Terrified I'm Going to Lose My Baby

Charlie, a client I had worked with several years ago, reached out to me during COVID for therapy regarding his high anxiety. He worked as a mechanic on airplanes. He had been off work for four weeks and was afraid of losing his job.

His nine-month-old infant son has had respiratory problems since birth. Charlie said he had spent numerous nights at the hospital with him and constantly feared losing him.

Over time, Charlie became increasingly more vigilant about his son's health. Even though he was taking all the necessary precautions, Charlie had become hyper-alert and couldn't work. Charlie was scaring himself with thoughts and images of his baby getting sick and dying. He was also afraid it would be his fault.

I worked with Charlie to realize what he was doing and to take responsibility for it. I taught him the difference between valid fear and irrational fear. I then coached him to interrupt his negative thoughts by staying with the sensations of fear and panic. I helped him focus on the sensations of fear as he experienced them and breathe through the waves as they rose, crested, and receded. As he did this, the sensations subsided. As the quality of the sensations became less intense and uncomfortable, Charlie calmed down and became more rational.

It took several weeks for him to develop the habit of breathing through the sensations of fear, but once he did, he felt in control, and he returned to work.

Exercise

Breathing Exercise:

Start with five seconds, then increase the time with each session.

- Pay attention to your breathing.

- Be aware of breathing in and notice the cool air entering your nostrils.

- Be aware of the warm air exiting your nostrils.

- Notice any sensations in your body. Do not try to change anything. There is no need to name or identify anything. Just *sense*.

- Be curious. What is, is.

- Catch yourself thinking.

- Shift to your body and notice the sensations. At first, you may not feel anything, so let it be. Let go of thinking about it.

- Stay with the numbness.

- As you continue to interrupt your thinking and shift to your body, you will start to notice sensations.

- Be curious. What is, is.

How to Help Others Help Themselves

Help others shift from thinking to sensing by asking about their feelings:

Ask questions that revolve around their feelings and not about the facts. The purpose of the questions is to elicit the sensations the person had experienced in the past and is experiencing in the present. People usually respond to these questions with explanations and more facts, and that is okay; keep listening and inquiring about their feelings. When they articulate their feelings, they become more aware, which they will find to be helpful.

Examples of questions:
(NOTE: None of the questions or statements below mention any facts.)

- When that happened, what impact did it have on you?

- When they said that to you, how did you feel?

- What was that like for you?

- How do you know when you feel disappointed? Where in your body are you experiencing sensations?

- When you found out, what was that like for you?

- Where in your body did you feel that?

- Did it feel more like a pain or an ache?

Examples of statements:

- Help me understand how you coped with that.

- Once again, run that by me.

- Walk me through how you felt during that. I want to know what it was like for you.

Key Takeaways:

- **The corpus callosum is a band of neurons that join the Logical Brain and the Sensory Brain.**

- **Deeply breathing facilitates the flow of Logical data and sensory data through the corpus callosum.**

- **New neural pathways form by synthesis and integration, creating new sensations.**

- **Holding the breath prevents the formation of new neural pathways.**

CHAPTER THREE

Breathe and Connect

"Awareness is the key to change." —Anonymous

Sometimes, when we hear something, see something, or think something, we hold our breath without realizing it. We go into the Logical Brain and think about it, question it, and analyze it, often disconnecting from our bodies. We often spend excessive amounts of time thinking, worrying, weighing the pros and cons, and scaring, doubting, and beating ourselves up. There is nothing wrong with thinking, but over-thinking, over-analyzing, and being too logical is not productive or healthy. What is important is the quality of our thinking. By changing the quality of our thinking (positive rather than negative), the meaning changes.

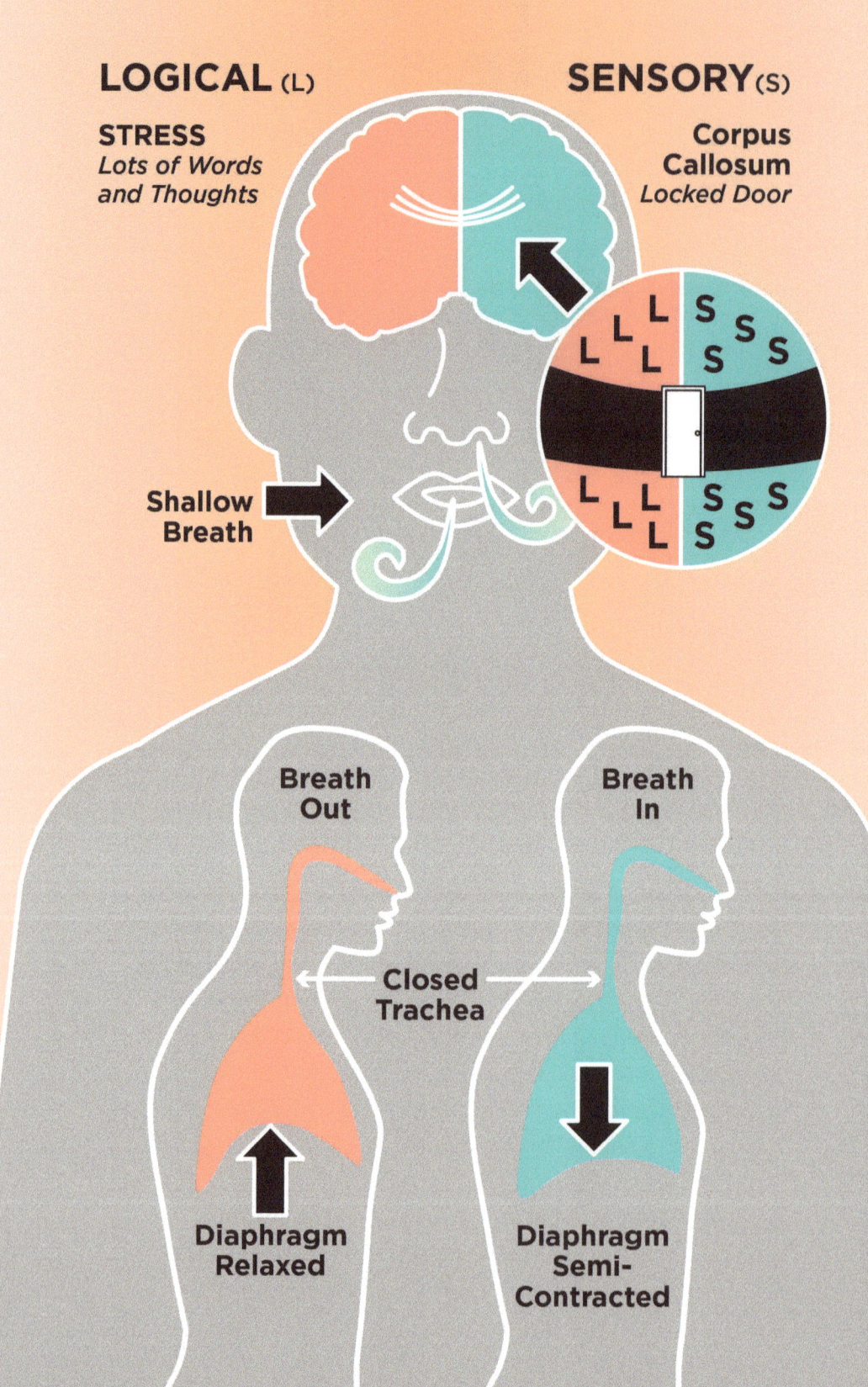

You can get into the Sensory Brain and stop over-thinking and analyzing everything by interrupting the Logical Brain.

Holding the breath and breathing shallow blocks the expression of emotions. This is a result of our Fight, Flight, Freeze response, and this happens when a person is afraid and adapts by *managing* emotions; they feel sensations and do not know what to do with them. The sensations increase because they cannot be *processed*, and then the person becomes more concerned, increasing the sensations even more and creating a vicious cycle. Fatigue, disappointment, discouragement, and other experiences give wear and tear on the person, and, therefore, people are more likely to meltdown or explode from the backlog of emotions.

Some people will often try indulging in all sorts of things to get respite from the sensations, like food, alcohol, medication, marijuana, etc. This might work, but not always. They might believe that the emotions need to be *managed* because they are always there in some form or another.

People are afraid of losing control if they stop *managing* their emotions. This is because they do not understand what is going on and how the Logical and Sensory brains work. People are ignorant about how their brains function. They think there is only one way to think—the way they do. If there is no awareness of how the brain works, there is no change. "I'm stuck with the way my brain works," or "I'm stuck with how I feel emotionally."

People often feel they are a victim of their emotions. Emotions seem unpredictable and confusing to them, making it harder to *manage* them. However, when people take respon-sibility for the emotions they experience, they can take charge of them. When people understand how their brains work and how to *process* emotions, they feel empowered and are not afraid of their brains (or emotions) anymore. As people experience positive changes from *processing* the sensations, control becomes a non-issue, just like breathing. People need to be re-taught what to do instead of *managing* their emotions.

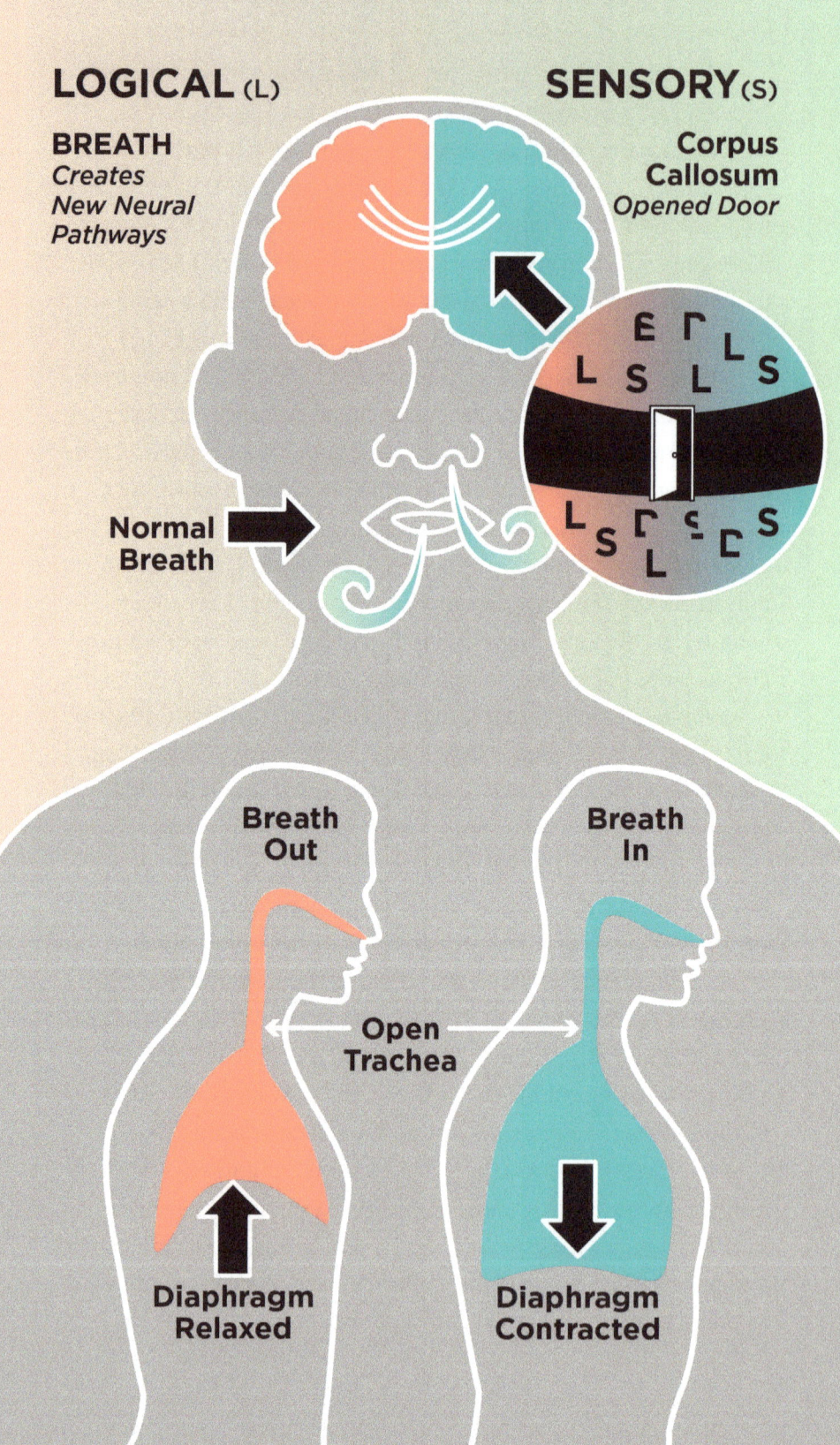

We are born knowing how to *process* emotions. Without language, infants have no thoughts, but they experience a bundle of sensations. Babies are born knowing how to cry because it is instinctual. They cry to communicate their needs—hunger, fatigue, comfort, connection, and attachment. The purpose of crying is to get their caregiver's attention. If the caregiver does not come and does not provide the child with what they need, the baby may not develop healthy ways of being.

When parents and other family members are happy, cuddly, and pay attention to their children, their children experience the sensations of pleasure, love, and connection. When they are distressed by events, such as interaction with an angry sibling, a frightening experience, or a parent leaving home, they feel the sensations of discomfort and pain, and their natural tendency is to cry. They cry fully and deeply in waves of sobs and wails that gradually get smaller until they are gone. Once they are gone, the child recovers quickly to their natural state. It often takes only a few minutes.

Crying is a genuine response to a distressing or overly positive situation, such as a child's disappointment when their toys are taken away or waves of gratitude when receiving a much-needed gift of money. The crying that is being referred to here is not manipulative. Manipulative crying is a different type of crying, which both children and adults often use.

It's Okay If I Cry

As two-year-old Joey was running his toy car on the furniture, he accidentally knocked over his mom's coffee. She yelled at him as she rushed to clean it up. He was startled and frightened by what happened. His mother's tone and facial expression distressed him. He cried fully and deeply. His little tummy expanded and contracted as his breath came in deep sobs. His cries came in waves. At first, his cries were loud and long until they became less intense. His mom hugged and reassured him. Gradually, his cries subsided and came to a natural halt. He quickly and easily went back to happily playing with his toy cars.

Not all expression of emotion involves crying. Sometimes, the expression of emotion may be sensations of fear/terror or intense sensations of love. The universe operates in waves, such as light waves, sound waves, heat waves, radio waves, etc. Emotions come in waves. An emotion wells up, crests, and then recedes. Then another wave—a smaller wave—rises, crests, and recedes. If the waves are not interrupted, they continue as long as the emotion/sensation lasts until there are no more waves, just like the waves reaching the ocean shore; they dissipate and are gone.

The breath is an integral part of this wave pattern. As the wave of sensations increases, the breath allows the flow of logical and sensory data through the corpus callosum. As the different types of data synthesize and integrate, new neural pathways form. The sensations are then *processed*, and there is nothing left to *manage*.

When people can fully express their emotions by breathing through the sensations, their personal energy stays aligned. People feel grounded because they stay connected to themselves. They can trust their emotions because they experience the sensations fully, meaning they do not avoid them. Because they can feel the range of sensations from peaceful to agitated and from ecstatic to despair, they feel a strong sense of aliveness. Thus, they heal from any emotional trauma they might have gone through or are currently experiencing.

As mentioned in Chapter 2, people learn to *manage* their emotions by holding their breath and/or breathing shallow, preventing the waves of sensations from cresting and receding. Here, part of the person's energy is trying to flow, and part is blocking the flow. The person's energy is opposed.

Interoception = Sensations = Affect

KEY

- ■ Terror
- |■| Fear/Insecurity
- [■] Safety/Security
- [■] Absolute Safety

- ∧∧∧∧ Ecstasy/Elation
- ∧∧∧ Happiness/ Joyfulness
- ∨∨∨ Sadness/Remorse
- — Deep Saddness/ Grief/Loss

- ⟷ Extreme Disgust/ Repulsion
- ⟨⟩ Disgust/Repulsion
- ✕ Attraction
- ⤫ Desire

- ◎ Deep Shame
- ⟲ Slight Shame/ Humiliation/ Embarrassment
- △ Pride
- ⧅ Extreme Pride
- ∞ Neutrality

As we grow up, we get messages about crying and other expressions of emotion from our family members, community, and culture. Somewhere along the path of growing up, children learn that expressing emotions is either welcome or not. Lucky are the children raised in homes and cultures where the expression of emotions is allowed and encouraged. They are coached on how to *process* their emotions by parents who model *processing* emotions. They develop many neural pathways for natural expression, enabling them to stay connected to themselves and others. Their energy is aligned and flowing in the same direction, and they can live life to the fullest.

Where Does It All Go Wrong?

What happens when families and cultures do not welcome the expression of emotion or only allow certain emotions to be expressed?

Parents either express or do not express their emotions. If parents suppress their emotions, their babies and toddlers copy them as they copy most things their parents or others do, such as mannerisms. When some children are very young, adults often scare, threaten, or train them to shut down the natural sequence of expression. When children are scared, they instinctively hold their breath and/or breath shallow until the real or imagined danger passes. They feel the sensations of terror, endure them, and try to survive them, or they freeze until the danger passes. They build many neural pathways for blocking and *managing* their emotions/sensations. This becomes a way of being—a habit—that helps them survive childhood. The problem is that they typically maintain this way of being into adulthood, and they often pass it on to their children.

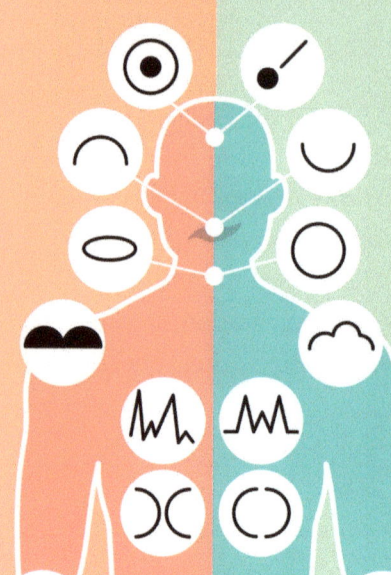

KEY

⊙	Migraine
⌒	Frown/ Pursed Lips/ Gritting Teeth
⬭	Lump in Throat/ Constricted Trachea
◗◖	Shoulders Heavy/ Stiff/Tight
⋀	Racing Heart/Chest Tightness
)(	Diaphragm Tightness/ Shallow/Rapid Breath
⋈	Intestinal Issues, Cramps
↗	Negative Sexual Urges/Sensations/Addiction
∿	Shaky/Tingly/Numb Arms
∿	Shaky/Tingly/Numb Legs
✳	Cold/Sore/Numb Feet

Therapeutic Headache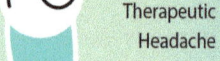

Smile/ Relaxed Mouth ⌣

Voice/Laughter/ Relaxed Trachea ○

Relaxed/Light Shoulders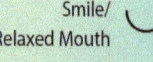

Positive Excitement/ Normal Heartbeat ⋀

Deep/Rhythmic Breath ( )

Positve Butterflies/ Good Digestion ❧

Positive Sexual Urges/Sensations ✳

Relaxed Arms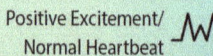

Strong/Balanced Legs ⬓

Warm/Steady Feet ◇

Parents and other adults treat children in many ways when they are uncomfortable expressing their emotions. They often get angry. They may shame, blame, judge, embarrass, humiliate, deflect, divert, minimize, stonewall, or name-call children—directly and indirectly—sending messages that expressing emotion is not acceptable and/or not tolerated. In turn, children assume they are bad.

When children are distressed, some parents make the situation worse by becoming more emotional than their children. Children learn that things get worse when they express emotion, so they shut themselves down. Children need their parents to be okay, so they may hide their emotions, often pretending they are okay when they are not. This, too, becomes a habit in childhood as they develop many neural pathways for blocking and shutting off. In adulthood, it becomes so familiar that it seems natural, but *it is not*. It is just a habit that has become ingrained.

I Don't Matter

Dina and Ruben sought counselling after many months of COVID-19 restrictions. Dina had lost her job at the spa, and Ruben was working from home. They had been struggling with their relationship for some time.

As I worked with them, I identified the problem in their dynamic. When Ruben would approach Dina with a relational problem, she would get upset and start crying. Ruben would then comfort and console her, reassuring her that everything between them was fine, even though it wasn't. In this way, Ruben never got his relational needs addressed because Dina was always too distressed to address his issue.

In our sessions, their dynamic would play out.

One day, when Ruben was comforting Dina, he experienced an epiphany— this was like his relationship with his mother. He said that as a child, whenever he got upset, his mother would feel sick, and he would have to take care of her. He learned to put himself aside and pretend he was okay so that she wouldn't get "sick" and he wouldn't get stuck looking after her. He frequently felt he didn't matter. He was now unconsciously playing out this dynamic with his wife.

This was new information for Ruben. It helped him understand why he often felt invisible and unacknowledged in the relationship. By recognizing what he was experiencing, I validated his experience. I then shifted the focus to Dina to explore her part in their dynamic.

Common Dynamic

When one partner gets flooded with intense, unpleasant sensations and cannot stay present when the couple interacts, it eventually results in the other partner concluding, "I do not matter."

This is a common dynamic between couples, and it can play out in different ways.

The partner who cannot stay present has few neural pathways for intimacy and closeness. This typically happens when childhood relationships with parents, grandparents, siblings, and other close relationships have been or remain difficult.

When men lack neural pathways for intimacy and closeness, they become flooded with intense, unpleasant sensations when approached by their partners to resolve emotional problems. They often push their partners away and treat their partners with contempt or get angry. They cannot stay present and engaged with their partners, so their partners feel that they do not matter.

When women lack neural pathways for intimacy and closeness, they tend to blame themselves, believing something is wrong with them when approached by their partners to resolve emotional problems. They often shut down and frequently get physically ill. They cannot stay present and engaged with their partners, so their partners feel that they do not matter.

When relationships are new, there is a lot of goodwill and love, so partners stop trying to get their needs met and instead shift their focus to comforting and reassuring their partners. Over time, this pattern repeats, and the result is the same: the partner cannot stay present and engaged; thus, the connection is lost.

UNPLEASANT

PLEASANT

KEY

Migraine

Frown/
Pursed Lips/
Gritting Teeth

Lump in Throat/
Constricted
Trachea

Shoulders Heavy/
Stiff/Tight

Racing Heart/Chest
Tightness

Diaphragm Tightness/
Shallow/Rapid Breath

Intestinal Issues, Cramps

Negative Sexual
Urges/Sensations/Addiction

Shaky/Tingly/Numb Arms

Shaky/Tingly/Numb Legs

Cold/Sore/Numb Feet

Therapeutic
Headache

Smile/
Relaxed Mouth

Voice/Laughter/
Relaxed Trachea

Relaxed/Light
Shoulders

Positive Excitement/
Normal Heartbeat

Deep/Rhythmic Breath

Positve Butterflies/
Good Digestion

Positive Sexual
Urges/Sensations

Relaxed Arms

Strong/Balanced Legs

Warm/Steady Feet

When people naturally access, express, and *process* their emotions, they behave in congruent ways. Depending on the context of a situation or their life circumstances, the emotion they experience and express will mostly be appropriate. However, even when people are congruent, they sometimes make mistakes, but when they do, they make them less often, and the mistakes they make are less grave. Plus, they are better at repairing any damage.

To some extent, we all *manage* our emotions. Some people seem to be unable to *manage* their emotions and instead spill their emotions all over others. Others *manage* their emotions to such an extent that they seem like robots or humanoids.

Emotional Containers

We all develop a style of how we express and *manage* our emotions/sensations. The style in which we do so is influenced by how safe or unsafe we felt growing up. Some people have a rigid style, while others are overly lax. Someone with a rigid style represses their emotions to such an extent that they no longer feel the emotions themselves, making it hard for others to connect with them, whereas someone with an overly lax style can burden others by spilling their emotions onto them.

The Therapeutic Container

A person can act as a therapeutic container for someone else's emotions. For example, as a therapist, I provide a therapeutic container for my clients by creating a safe environment and connecting with them. In the *process*, I let clients know they are

**Jot down your ideas,
memories, sensations.**

in control and they do not have to do (or not do) anything they do not want to do. Furthermore, I must provide an environment where what my clients say and do remains confidential **(except for information I am required to report by law—clients who are a danger to themselves or others).**

Occasionally, early in therapy, new clients often tell me that they trust me. In these instances, I inform them that it is too early to trust me and that they need to let me earn their trust. This teaches them to have stronger boundaries to protect themselves from me and others.

Often, clients are not truthful at first. However, this is part of the *process* of building the therapeutic relationship. When they trust me and are ready to face what they need to face, they start speaking their truth. So, I'm okay with clients lying to me because I know that when they are ready, they will be truthful. Often too, clients are not ready to admit to themselves their truth.

When clients experience safety and connect with me, they begin to share their stories and express their sensations. They begin to let go of their containers and allow me to be a container for them. When they let go, they can feel their sensations more deeply. I listen intently, support and encourage them, and validate their emotions and experiences.

I educate my clients about emotions, reframe the content, and fully engage in the *process* with them. Often, when clients experience deep emotional sensations, I help them notice the sensations they are experiencing in their bodies (pleasant/ unpleasant, agitated, excited, and calm), and I help them to stay with the sensations longer and breathe through them. Sometimes, I want to facilitate their *processing* by sitting beside them and rubbing their back. I always ask for permission to do this. I let them know that they could tell me to stop at any time. This is

the only time the container becomes physical. In this way, I am providing a therapeutic container for them.

One of the problems of COVID-19 restrictions is that I cannot approach the client as per social distancing measures. Furthermore, videoconferencing does not allow me to do this either. So, what I do when I feel the urge to connect is that I tell them that if it weren't for the COVID-19 restrictions, I would ask for permission to sit beside them and rub the center of their back. They are often grateful to know that I care about connecting with them.

In this healing *process*, people need to let go of their own containers to go to the depth of their feelings and the intensity of their sensations. They need someone to trust and someone who is emotionally strong to "hold them" while they go through the *process*. It is very scary to go into the depths of despair (or other heavy emotion/sensation) alone. If we are with loved ones who are not solid themselves, we tend to hold ourselves back because we want to protect them from our emotional pain or because we know they can't handle it. Thus, we put our pain aside to look after them.

As children grow up, they develop emotional containers; they are not born with them intact. They need to develop them over time. They have urges and impulses that they learn to control, and often, they need their parents to be their emotional containers.

Sometimes, they need the emotional container to be physical, like when a father holds his extremely distraught son. How and when parents contain their children's emotions shapes the development of the child. When parents contain in a firm and loving way, children feel safe, loved, and that they matter. When parents contain in a harsh way, children feel unsafe and unloved and that they do not matter. A child's natural spirit can be crushed and annihilated, or it can be nourished and cherished.

Healthcare Burnout

Kamila has been a client of mine intermittently for about ten years. She works as a nurse in a large hospital. When Kamila came in with her husband for a couple's session, I quickly realized that she was not herself. Instead of focusing on her marital relationship, she talked about the patients in her ward, saying she was concerned about their level of care.

I could tell she was exhausted but did not realize it. She looked and acted like a zombie. I reflected back to her, "You seem exhausted." She ignored my feedback and kept talking about the drop in the level of care at the hospital. I continued to listen to her and kept reflecting back to her, "You seem tired." She continued to focus on her concerns at the hospital. By the sixth time I caringly told her that she seemed exhausted, she finally broke down and started sobbing deeply. I suggested that her husband, who was concerned and shocked by the depth of her crying, put his hand on the middle of her back and gently rub it in small circles. He willingly complied. I then continued to reflectively listen to Kamila about her concern for her patients as I knew how important it was to her. She needed me, or at least someone, to validate her concern. As I did that, she let go and sobbed to the depths. Typically, she'd act as her own emotional container, but in this case, she did not need to because she knew I was there and could handle her deep emotion. I facilitated her expression of emotion as she cried through the waves of sensations.

At the end of the session, I told her I would contact her doctor and recommend that she take time off. She looked at me through her fatigue with relief in her eyes. I reassured her that I would tell her doctor that I was not worried about her level of care for her patients but that I was concerned she would risk her own physical and emotional health by taking care of others.

I told her husband that she would be exhausted after our session and for the next few weeks, so he would need to ensure that she got a lot of rest. He looked relieved as well as he knew she was overtired, but he was at a loss of what to do.

I contacted her family physician, and he put her on medical leave for four weeks. She is back at work again now and is doing okay.

The Importance of Having a Support System

For many of us, too much thinking inside our heads can lead to distortion. Sometimes, even saying what you think out loud without anyone hearing helps develop awareness. It helps to recognize distortion and/or healthy thinking/ideas. Having someone to talk to and use as a sounding board is very helpful. Talking to someone you trust to keep what you say/think in confidence will help you go deeper within yourself since you do not have to protect yourself. In addition, doing this work with a competent therapist who has your best interests at heart supports and encourages permanent therapeutic change.

You and anyone in your support system need to know that shifting from *managing* the sensations of emotions to *processing* the sensations of emotions takes time. However, once *processing* becomes a habit, it goes more quickly. Getting there may take some time because we hate to let go of the ways of being that helped us survive childhood and even part of adulthood.

When people are emotionally healthy, they can be their own containers in constructive ways because they know how to *process* emotions. They typically do not need anyone to hold them or be a container for them emotionally—they eventually learn to do this for themselves through practice. However, it can still feel wonderful to be held emotionally and/or physically by a loved one or trusted friend.

Exercise

Connect with yourself at the depths, go to the edges, and come back. Make sure to find an appropriate time and place to access your emotions so that you will not be interrupted.

- Shift out of the Logical Brain (interrupt thinking).

- Focus on your breath.

- Take your time (the Sensory Brain works more slowly than the Logical Brain).

- Imagine your pain as a dark blob or mass.

- Allow yourself to go to the edges of the mass.

- Allow the unpleasant sensations to come more into your awareness.

- Breathe into the sensations for three to five seconds.

- Now, let the mass float away.

- Breathe.

- Rest.

- Repeat for ten seconds.

- Now, let the sensations float away.

- Breathe.

- Repeat for fifteen seconds.

- Stop when you want or before it gets to be too much, and plan another time to heal yourself.

Every time you do this, you will be able to go deeper and deeper. As you *process* the emotional sensations, the mass will become smaller, and it will become easier until your personal energy is aligned.

How to Help Others Help Themselves

Comforting a person in emotional pain by rubbing their back:

- Only offer to rub someone's back if you want to and if you feel okay doing so.

- Let the distressed person know that you want to rub their back and say, "I want to sit beside you and rub the center of your back. Would you be okay with this?"

- Let the person know that if they are uncomfortable, they can tell you to stop.

- Once permission is obtained, sit next to them and slowly rub the center of their back (DO NOT touch them anywhere else, i.e., stroke their hair, the sides of their body, their lower back, etc.).

- Ensure the person has access to tissues, but let them handle their physical expression on their own.

- Occasionally, check with them to see if they want you to continue rubbing their back and move away if they do not. "Are you okay with me still rubbing your back?"

- Eventually, say to them, "I'm going to stop now. Are you okay with that?"

- If they are okay, move away. If not, continue.

- At some point, it will come to a natural end.

Be patient when you do this, as it can take a while. If you need to go or you have had enough, you can inform the person that you are going to stop.

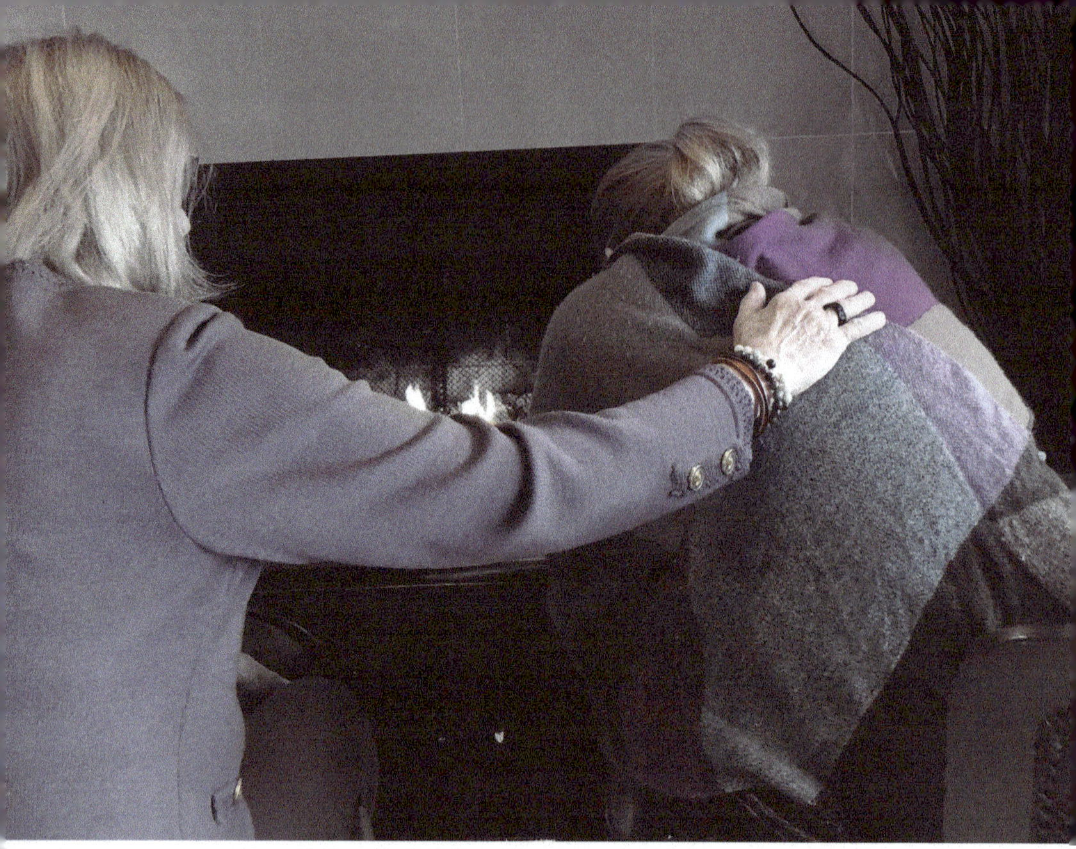

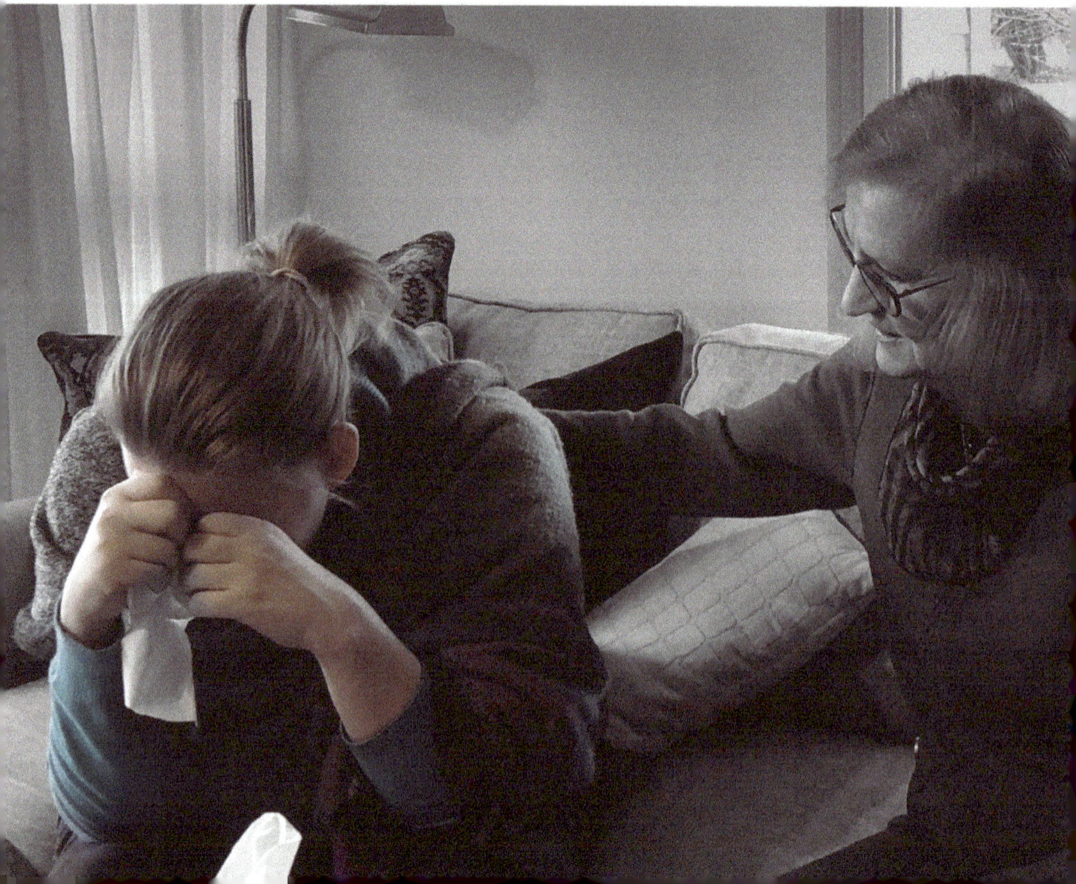

Key Takeaways:

- Emotions come in waves.

- Breathing through the sensations of emotions is the key to *processing* them.

- It's important to develop one's own emotional container.

CHAPTER FOUR

Manage Less, Process More

"Let go of the outcome." —Anonymous

Oh! Now I Know What to Do

Giving birth to my first child left me feeling physically and emotionally exhausted for the first time in my life. After a complicated birth, I came home from the hospital and expected to carry on just as I had before. I was hyper-vigilant with my new baby and was sleep-deprived. About ten days later, I broke down sobbing and couldn't stop. I didn't know what was happening to me. Eventually, I realized I was experiencing total exhaustion. Of course, I felt exhausted, but since I hadn't felt that way before, I didn't know what I was feeling at first.

That first experience of exhaustion taught me that there are cues, in the form of sensations, that I can now use to monitor my degree of fatigue. I learned that when my left eyelid starts twitching, I know I'm tired and need to rest. If I'm more tired, I get a specific form of nausea. When I get these sensations, I know I must rest, or I can't function properly.

Understanding what these sensations mean has proved helpful. I use them as my guide to know when I need to rest so that I never get to the point of exhaustion again.

It's normal to feel sensations we've never felt before and not recognize them. We learn about specific emotions from others by talking about them, from reading books, listening to podcasts, and watching movies and TV. It's one thing to know something intellectually, yet entirely another to know it experientially. The more we can recognize, understand, and feel sensations, the better they can serve as our guide.

Most people do not understand emotions. They do not know how they are created. They tend to think they are arbitrary and unpredictable. People talk about their emotions as if they are conditions or a state-of-being. For example, "My anxiety is so high I can't go out tonight." Sometimes they even see them as illnesses. For example, "I've been suffering from depression for half my life." They do not realize that anxiety and depression are symptoms of their way of being in life. They are *managing* the symptoms instead of addressing the cause of their symptoms. They see doctors in hopes of getting help, but they often just get medications to treat their symptoms rather than the cause of their symptoms.

Understanding what these sensations mean has proved helpful. I use them as my guide to know when I need to rest so that I never get to the point of exhaustion again.

The Oxford dictionary defines emotion as:

- a strong feeling deriving from one's circumstances, mood, or relationships with others.

- an instinctive or intuitive feeling as distinguished from reasoning or knowledge.

The definition above does not include any mention of sensations in regards to emotions; however, I believe that sensations are at the root of emotional *processing*.

We can experience a range of different emotions, also called feelings. Some of these include happy, calm, peaceful, angry, abandoned, powerless, out-of-control, hopeless, irritated, shameful, cozy, loved, connected, delighted, spiritual, hopeful, lustful, goofy, detached, ecstatic, dreamy, inspired, hurt, and many more.

Some emotions are common, such as sadness, hurt, happiness, embarrassment, and excitement, while others are rarer, such as ecstasy, despair, emotional exhaustion, and abject terror. We experience each emotion on a level of intensity, ranging from slight to intense.

Emotions Are Like Constellations of Stars in the Sky

To understand emotions, I look to the stars. There are millions of stars in the sky. No matter where we are in the universe, the stars stay in the same place, even if our view or perspective of them is different. Travellers have used stars to help guide them on their journeys for centuries. To understand and talk about the stars, we have organized them into groups called constellations and have given them individual names—Big Dipper, Small Dipper, Orion, Cassiopeia. The good news is that we do not need to know everything about the universe to use the stars as our guides.

Breathe through the sensations.

Naming the Constellations of Emotions

- Emotions: umbrella of feeling states.

- Feelings: feeling states comprising specific constellations of sensations.

- Sensations: sensory data from our senses—sight, hearing, smell, taste, and touch (this includes images and memories).

We have proprioceptors in our muscles, which inform us where our body parts are. We have extrasensory perception, often called the sixth sense, which helps us detect information from the universe through telepathy or clairvoyance.

I define emotion as:

- a unique constellation of sensations grouped together and experienced in the Sensory Brain, limbic system, and body.

- a feeling state that informs us: a) we are alive, and that we are living, breathing organisms, and b) we are humans and not robots.

- intuitive or instinctive as opposed to logical and rational.

Personal Story—Joy

Years ago, I lived in a home and had my office in one half of my garage, so I'd go back and forth between the house and the garage. One time, as I was going out to the garage, I was struck by the beauty of the yellow daffodils planted outside the garage. The beauty of the daffodils was so powerful that it broke through my focus on work and filled me with JOY.

MEMORIAL BENCH

Personal Story—Grief

When my son died, I couldn't cry or express my grief for some time. Forty days later, at a gathering to honour him, I put my head down on the table and wept in anguish for some time through waves of sensations. Someone came and rubbed my back. I don't know who it was, but I was grateful. I felt relief afterwards, and I thawed out.

Much like constellations, we label the feeling state to identify it, talk about it, and understand it. Like the stars in the universe, we need not know everything about the brain, mind, and body to use the sensations as our guide.

As children grow up, they learn to name their bodily sensations. They discover that certain sensations mean they need to pee, while others mean they need to poop. There are sensations for thirst, hunger, tiredness, sickness, dizziness, and feeling satisfied or full. When they feel sensations of pain, children understand they are physically hurt or sick.

In the same way, children learn to name different constellations of emotions. They discover that certain emotions mean they feel sad, excited, left out, emotionally hurt, emotionally satisfied, prized, disappointed, and angry, among others.

Each feeling state has a behavioural or non-verbal expression. For example:

- Joy is a constellation of pleasant sensations we experience as uplifting and happy. "Jumping for joy" is the behavioural action (or expression) that often accompanies great joy.

- Grief is a constellation of emotionally painful sensations we experience as a loss. Wailing, sobbing, and crying are expressions of grief. Pounding one's body, rocking, and listlessness are behavioural actions that often accompany grief.

FEAR

FEAR

**Nervous-Apprehensive,
A Little Scared**

A Little Worried

A Little Anxious

**Abject Terror,
Blackout**

Worried Sick

**Highly Anxious,
Panic**

Many Shades of Fear

We have learned to label groups of sensations using the Logical Brain. Until children learn the name of certain constellations of sensations, they do not understand what they feel. Even though children are aware they feel something, they do not know what to call it. For example, as we experienced sensations of tears welling up in our eyes and sensations in our throat and chest, we learned to call this constellation of sensations "sadness."

Many of us, particularly children, cannot identify what we are feeling; we just know we feel pleasant/unpleasant/intense/calm. While we do not need to name or identify a specific emotion to experience or *process* it, most of us like to understand what is happening since we believe/think that we make better decisions when we recognize what is going on. Often the unpleasant sensations do not change even though we understand what's causing them.

Same Emotion, Different Names

Different names can be given to some constellations of sensations yet capture different intensities of the same emotion. "Fearful" has several words or terms that identify the same feeling: appre-hensive, nervous, worried, scared, anxious, afraid, panic-stricken, frightened, terrified, and blackout (so terrified that a person dissociates). These names describe different qualities of the same emotion: FEAR.

FEDERER LOSES

Photo by Ben Lewis — Rafael Nadal defeats Roger Federer in the Men's Singles Final at Australian Tennis Open at Melbourne Park on February 1, 2009

FEDERER WINS

Photo by Frank Molter — Roger Federer wins 20th Grand Slam title at 2018 Australian Open at Melbourne Park

Similar Sensations, Different Feelings

Some feelings are confusing because they appear to be similar. Some sensations between sadness and disappointment are the same, but disappointment has slightly different constellations of sensations. It is possible to be sad and disappointed, or sad and not disappointed, or disappointed and not sad.

Most of the time, we can identify the emotion. "I'm feeling disappointed, not sad," or "I'm feeling disappointed and a little sad," or "I'm not disappointed, just sad."

To access each feeling, we must separate sensations from each constellation. To *process*, we must stay with the sensations of disappointment and breathe through them. The sensations come in waves and gradually dissipate. Next, we must stay with the sensations of sadness and *process* them by breathing through them.

Feeling sad and emotionally "touched" or "moved" have a similar expression—teary, crying, sobbing—yet are opposite in meaning. Sadness is typically unpleasant while feeling "moved" or "touched" is pleasant. Consider Olympic athletes who win a medal and how they often show emotions that look like those exhibited by someone who has experienced a loss.

The clarity that comes from knowing what we are experiencing is satisfying. Accessing sensations to the depths feels powerful, which is the opposite of feeling powerless. Knowing how to *process* feelings is extremely helpful and productive.

**Jot down some memories
that come to mind.**

Experiencing Many Feelings at Once

It is possible to experience many feelings at once. New parents are often flooded with different feelings. They are excited, happy, and frightened by the enormous responsibility of caring for a child and overwhelmed, concerned, and awed by the tiny new being they have created.

It is also possible to experience opposing feelings simultaneously. Lottery winners often feel excited and discombobulated because their lives have turned upside down. Another example is feeling bittersweet. An hour after putting down my beloved fifteen-year-old cat, I was holding my first newborn grandchild. I felt grief at the loss of my cat and joy with the new baby in my arms.

We can also experience an assortment of jumbled feelings—a cocktail of emotions. We may say we feel "a bit off," "down in the dumps," "on edge," or "jumpy." These are global feelings, and typically, they show a lack of awareness. To understand which ingredients are in the cocktail, we need to access the sensations and sense them for a few seconds or minutes. As we stay with the sensations by being mindful and aware of them, we gather more data from the constellation of each feeling. With the increased sensory data, the feelings differentiate from each other.

When we notice what we are feeling and embrace our sensations, we can experience all the sensations for each emotion. Then we can feel the range of emotions—pleasant and unpleasant—slight to intense, and feel fully alive and engaged in living our life. Our awareness increases as we access the constellation of sensations for each feeling.

Conflicted

In a session, a client told me that her husband was very worried about her health. He thought she was working too hard. She said she didn't think so, but she was not sure. I had her focus on her inner conflict. I asked her to sit in one chair facing another chair. I directed her to imagine she was having a conversation with herself. She immediately saw her yellow tabby cat, Silke, curled up happily, napping. I asked her to move to the other chair and pretend to be her cat and told her to notice what sensations she felt. As she imagined she was Silke, she laughed and said, "I love to work. I'm like Silke; I can nap and jump up and go to work whenever I want. I know I'm okay, but my husband is worried."

I told her that now that she was clear within herself, she would be clearer with her husband. Then I added, "Maybe he is missing you."

Healthy Appropriate Actions Precipitate from Awareness

If we understand what we are experiencing, we are more likely to take appropriate action if we choose to act. When we fully know ourselves and our circumstances, we are naturally more spontaneous and can trust the steps we may spontaneously take.

Pay attention to your sensations (sensory data includes images, dreams, fantasies, and memories). Much like the stars helped explorers know their position on the planet and guided them on their journeys, your emotions are your guide to how you are at any moment. They may indicate you need to do something, such as take care of yourself, or confirm you are handling things in a way that works or not. They may indicate you need to stop going in one direction and shift to another, or you may get an insight into your situation, which gives you a new perspective that rings true for you.

What is more, when you clearly understand what you are experiencing, you can also interact with others more authentically because you can articulate what you need or how you are feeling. It is difficult to understand or interact with those who are unclear about what they feel. Misinterpretation leads to decisions that create mistaken beliefs, which leads to decisions that take a person in the wrong direction, hurt relationships, or cause problems at work. With clarification on what you are sensing and feeling, you can avoid misunderstandings.

We can be aware of our emotions, feelings, and sensations in our bodies or detach from them.

*Let go of
the outcome.*

Oh! I've Got to Figure Myself Out First

Bruno was a client of mine who worked for a large tech company as a senior engineer. He was divorced from his wife and lived with his partner, Lacy. He had a preteen daughter, and he and Lacy had an 18-month-old toddler.

As the baby got older, the pressure of childcare exacerbated their relationship issues to the point where Lacy brought up separating. Bruno, who didn't want to break up, reached out to me for therapy.

Bruno told me his story. He loved his work; he loved the challenge of solving problems. He said he would get lost in his work and "live in his head," forgetting about everything, and often worked 18-hour days. Lacy worked in the HR department at the same company. They no longer had a nanny, and Lacy felt resentful about doing most of the childcare.

Bruno said Lacy kept wanting something from him, but he didn't know what it was.

I explored Bruno's childhood with him. He said his father ruled the family with an iron fist—acting up or acting out weren't options. Bruno said he became very good at listening to his father and figuring out what his father wanted and didn't want. However, he didn't realize that he had to detach from his body and mind to do so. He learned not to question, try to reason, think for himself, or feel.

Therefore, in all areas of his life, he played out the same dynamic that he learned in childhood—to figure out what others want and need and make that happen. This is why he was good at his job—he figured out what his bosses wanted and worked hard to make it happen, disconnecting from himself in the process.

Similarly, he tried to figure out what his wife wanted, but he didn't know how to behave in a way that met her needs.

*Let things
fall together.*

I worked with Bruno to reconnect with himself. We started by interrupting his thinking and doing a scan of his body for sensations. At first, he didn't feel anything; he was numb. However, I was gradually able to bring to his awareness the sensations he was experiencing at the moment. I encouraged and coached him to breathe into whatever sensations he was having. However, he could only stay with the sensations for a few seconds at a time. Frequently, he would say, "I do not know what I'm supposed to be looking for." I told him to shift from trying to figure it out with logic to sensing the sensations in his body—to be curious about the sensations and to let go of why he was feeling them.

I helped him see that he was doing what his father taught him to do—control the outcome—in all aspects of his life. To do that, he had to detach from his body and mind. I told him to let go of the outcome, which was a new concept for him. He had not realized that he had been trying to control the outcome his entire life. Knowing this deconstructed his modus operandi for life, he was both ecstatic and relieved. His creativity could blossom.

In ongoing therapy, I helped him focus on his wants, needs, standards, and values. As emotions and feelings came up, I coached him to stay with them and breathe through the sensations. Since he didn't have many experiences of emotional closeness, he often got uncomfortable with extended times of intimacy. I advised him not to fight with Lacy when he got uncomfortable but to tell her that he needed a break instead.

As he became more aware of himself, he began to connect with Lacy in mutually satisfactory ways. He finally understood what she wanted from him— connection.

Accessing Emotions

Clients often say to me, "I do not know what I'm feeling." They say this because they are afraid of the sensations and have partially detached from them or cannot identify them. Most of us get a twinge—a few sensations from a constellation of a feeling—and quickly shift into the Logical Brain to diagnose the feeling and try to figure out why we are experiencing it.

When clients do this, I guide them from thinking/analyzing to sensing. I tell them to let go of the need to know. I use a metaphor to explain that they need to change how they handle their feelings. "When you try to figure out what you're feeling with the Logical Brain, it's like trying to enter a house repeatedly through a locked front door without a key. When you access and breathe through the sensations, it's like going through the back door that's unlocked."

In cities, the constellations of stars are harder to see because of the city lights, making it difficult to identify them. However, in the countryside, where there are fewer or no lights, it is much easier to see all the stars that make up each constellation. To see the stars, we need to turn off the lights. In the same way, to know what we feel, we need to "turn off" the Logical Brain and focus on the sensations (images and memories). We pay attention to and get curious about whatever sensations we are aware of by feeling, experiencing, and breathing through them.

As we stay with the sensations, we access more of the constellation of whatever emotion we are experiencing. The more sensations we access, the more we feel that emotion, and the more we feel that emotion, the more sensations we access—until we get them all. This gives us the data we need in a non-verbal form. Once we have more data, we can name it.

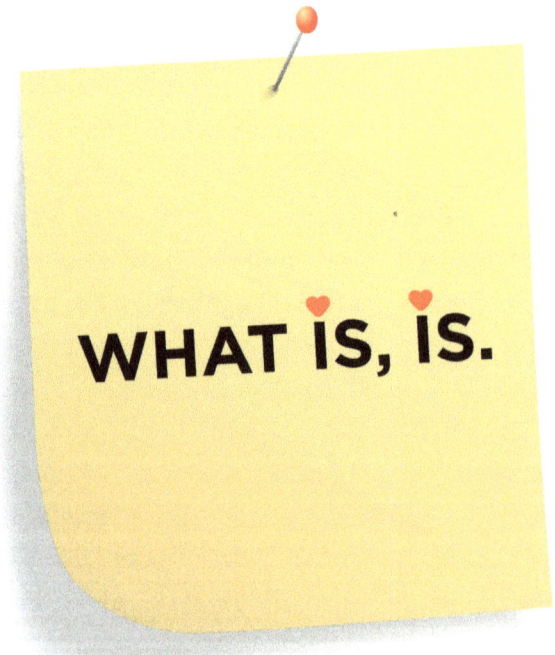

"What am I feeling?"

The answer to your question is not in the Logical Brain; it is in your Sensory Brain (limbic system and body).

First, shift to your Sensory Brain by making a statement: I am feeling something. Then, scan your body for sensations, and be curious about the sensations—where are they in your body? Are they high/low, strong/weak, blue/or some other colour? Are they tight/loose, stringy/spongy? There are no right or wrong sensations. Stay with them and breathe through them.

As you access more and more sensations and breathe through them, your brain will integrate the sensations with the facts (Logical Brain). *The answer will be revealed to you.* You will intellectually know what you are feeling, and you will experientially know what you are feeling. One type of knowledge confirms the other. You will feel grounded.

Accessing: "What Is, Is."

Staying with what you are sensing in the here and now is an effective way to access experiential data. It is a productive way to access what is helpful to know.

Accessing and breathing through the sensations in the here and now is known as *processing*. To analyze the who, what, when, where, why, and how is not relevant or productive *at this point*. In fact, it gets in the way and impedes accessing/*processing*.

It is essential to know that while becoming clear on a feeling can help us know which action to take or not when it comes to accessing, it does not matter what the feeling is or what you call it. If you are experiencing a feeling, it does not matter if you are experiencing a different feeling than someone else or whether the feeling you are experiencing is valid or not. When accessing a feeling, it is imperative to remember: "What is, is."

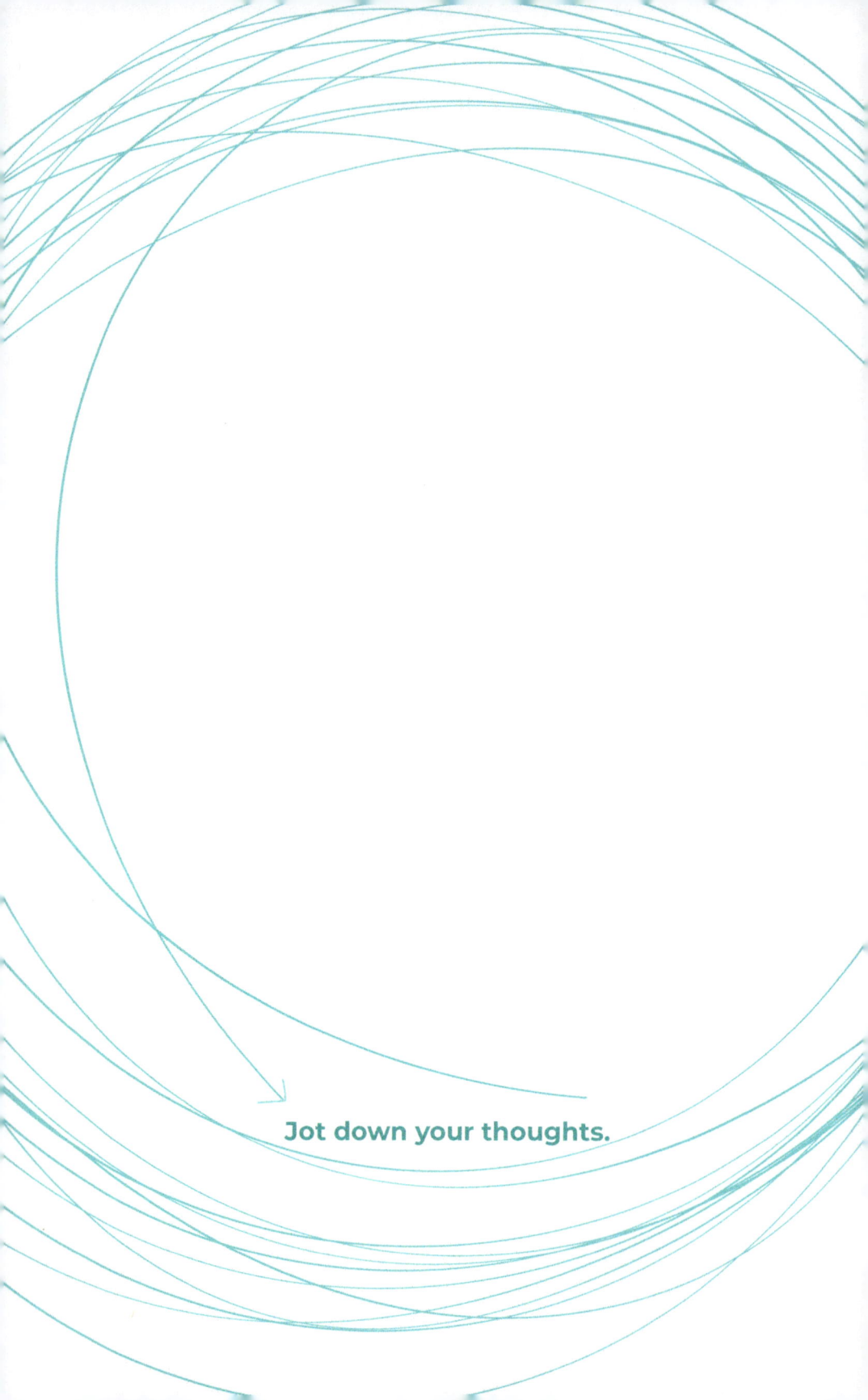

Jot down your thoughts.

Let's say you are feeling abandoned. Access the sensations of abandonment and breathe through them. As you breathe through the sensations, your brain will synthesize the facts with sensory data, and afterward, you will feel differently—either less bad or a lot better. Later, if you find out you were wrong (you were not feeling abandoned; you were simply tired), it does not matter. You needed to *process* what you were experiencing at that moment to get to a different accurate psychological state.

Awareness of Self

Without awareness, therapeutic/healthy change is unlikely. Our body is continually sending millions of pieces of information to our brain to make us aware, and our skin is the largest organ in our body. The following exercise will help you connect with the sensations in your body.

Exercise

Awareness Exercise

- Sit down. Turn your attention to your body. Take a breath. The Sensory Brain works more slowly than the Logical Brain.

- Focus on sensations—hot/cold, loose/tight, hard/soft, agitated/calm, pleasant/unpleasant, etc.

- Start with your feet: wiggle your toes, raise your heels.

- If you are wearing shoes, feel the sensations on your feet, and now, your socks.

- Shift your focus on sensations in your shins, calves, and knees.

- Move up to your lower body. Notice the sensations of your buttocks and your back on the seat.

- Notice any sensations from your genitals, stomach, and intestines.

- Notice the surface you are sitting on—is it soft, hard, wood, cloth?

- Notice the sensations.

- Notice your back—is it leaning against something, or is it free?

- What sensations do you feel in your lower back and upper back?

- Shift to your chest. Notice any sensations in your upper torso, heart, lungs, etc.

- Shift to your neck. What sensations do you feel around your neck? Is it free, or do you have clothing around it?

- Shift to your head, your scalp, and your face—is it tight or relaxed?

- Shift to inside your head. Are there any sensations of aches or pain, excitement, or peacefulness?

- Take a breath.

To become aware, you need to interrupt the Logical Brain thinking and shift to the Sensory Brain sensing.

As you continue to implement these new behaviours, you will increase the time you spend sensing. The more time you spend sensing, the more sensations you will notice and become aware of. The more sensations you get and the more time you spend in the Sensory Brain, the better your brain will synthesize logical data with experiential data, creating new neural pathways. New neural pathways create new ideas, perceptions of circumstances and situations, new sensations, solve problems, etc.

Increase the time you stay with the sensations. With every increase, you will be able to stay in your Sensory Brain, limbic system, and body for increasingly longer times. This is restful and restorative.

Personal Story— I Wish I Had Handled That Differently

When my son was fifteen years old, I made a big mistake when he told me about an early memory he had at the age of four.

He recalled the time we took a family trip to Hawaii, and he was swarmed by red ants on the beach, remembering that he was alone and there was no one around to help him.

His recollection was far from the truth.

I remembered the incident well. We went to Hawaii when he was two and a half years old, not four, and it happened when we were returning from grocery shopping. We had parked the car on the sidewalk, which was covered in sand, near our rental home. We weren't on the beach.

As my husband and I were unloading the groceries, my son started screaming. We quickly ran to him, my husband lifted him up, and I brushed the red ants off his feet. He was not alone.

When he told me this, I reacted strongly and with intensity. Instead of reflective listening, I needed him to understand that I was a good mom and that we were there for him. He then shut down because I invalidated his experience. What I should have done is not make it about me. Instead, I should have let it be his story and experience. I should have forgotten about the facts and should have just listened. Sometime later, I could have shared my experience of the event with him, not to show him that he was wrong, but to reassure him that I was there for him.

How to Help Others Help Themselves

Helping others *process* their emotions:

When someone is talking to you, let go of thinking whether the facts are accurate. Right now, it does not matter whether the facts are accurate; this is about reflective listening. What matters is their perception of the facts and their experience—the sensations they feel in this moment. Allow them to experience them fully.

Slow down their pace by telling them that what they are saying is important. Tell them how you are impacted by what they are saying, i.e., "I get goosebumps as you tell me that."

Key Takeaways:

- Awareness is knowing what you are experiencing.

- Each emotion has its own constellation of sensations.

- To *process* an emotion, you need to stay with the sensations.

CHAPTER FIVE

Change and Rearrange

"Slow down, you'll get there faster." —Anonymous

Emotions are influenced by perception, and perception influences emotions. This chapter teaches us how the brain makes meaning out of data and how meaning influences emotion.

Meaning often changes when we get more information, reframe information, and when there are changes in sensations.

Making Meaning

Our brain is constantly creating new neural pathways on a small to large scale, working hard to make meaning from every aspect of our lives. This is instinctual, programmed into our DNA from centuries of survival. Typically, this is done on so small a scale that we are unaware of it. People are so focused on making sense of things that they rarely feel their brains working. I want you to *feel* your brain working.

Different Ways to Make Meaning

1. Filling in the Gaps

Since we rarely have all the information or data that we need to make meaning, the brain fills in the gaps—sometimes accurately and sometimes inaccurately.

Look at the figure on the left. Notice the sensations in your brain as you look at it.

Feel your brain trying to make meaning out of it and notice how quickly your brain connects the strokes and "sees" the horse. Notice the sensations you experience as you "get it," i.e., make meaning.

This *process* of filling in the gaps happens all the time, so we rarely notice the physical sensations in our brain as it happens, plus we tend to stay focused on the meaning made in those moments.

AHA! !! !

Personal Story—I Love That Feeling!

I was learning geometry in Grade 9 and struggling with the theorems.
Suddenly, I "got it." The sensations in my head were so intense and
satisfying that I remember the moment to this day.

Only when the sensations in our brain are intense enough do we notice them, like when we have one of those "aha moments." This happens when we suddenly realize something, learn something important, have an idea, or get the gist of a joke. Another expression people use to describe this experience is: "It was like a lightbulb turned on in my head."

It is difficult to explain this experience in words, so we use the lightbulb metaphor to express what happened. When a lightbulb goes on, it sheds light on things, enabling us to see/know things we could not see/know before.

The Brain at Work

When we pay attention, we can feel our brain working and creating new neural pathways.

People believe we all experience life the same way, but we all have a different take on it; we put the data together in different ways based on who we are and our past and current experiences, as well as the sensations we have at the moment, and we then make different meaning out of them.

What do you see?

If you see a woman, you are right. Is she young or old? If you said "young," you are right. If you said "old," you are right. If you said "both," you are also right.

Even when we are given the same data, we can see different things and make different meaning out of it. It is important for us to know that we can all be presented with the same data but make an entirely different meaning from it. If you and I have different takes on an issue and I cannot see the meaning you make and you cannot see the meaning I make, we will have difficulty relating to each other. If we need to resolve something, we may not be able to, or it might be very difficult to resolve. However, if you see what I see and I see what you see, we can relate to each other and connect. Resolving is much easier when we see or "get" both sides of an issue.

Rigid and Flexible Thinking

Flexible thinking occurs when the mind lets go of the meaning made and can see the same data/situation/circumstances differently.

Rigid thinking occurs when the mind locks onto a meaning and cannot let go of it.

Look at the image on the left again. Remember, it is black marks on a white background. If you can only see one woman, i.e., the young woman, try to let go of that image and see whether you can let your mind "see" the old woman. In other words, try to "un-see" what you automatically see. If you cover up part of the image, it may help you let go of the meaning your mind initially made, enabling you to see the old woman.

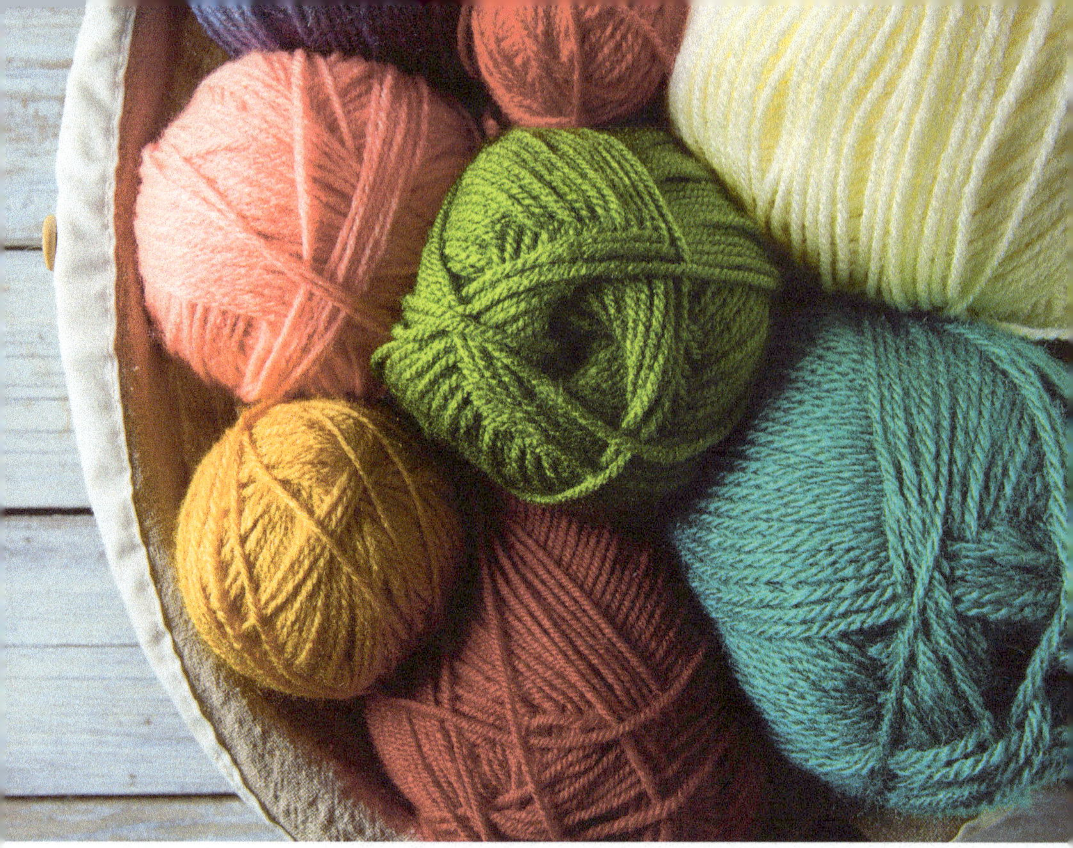

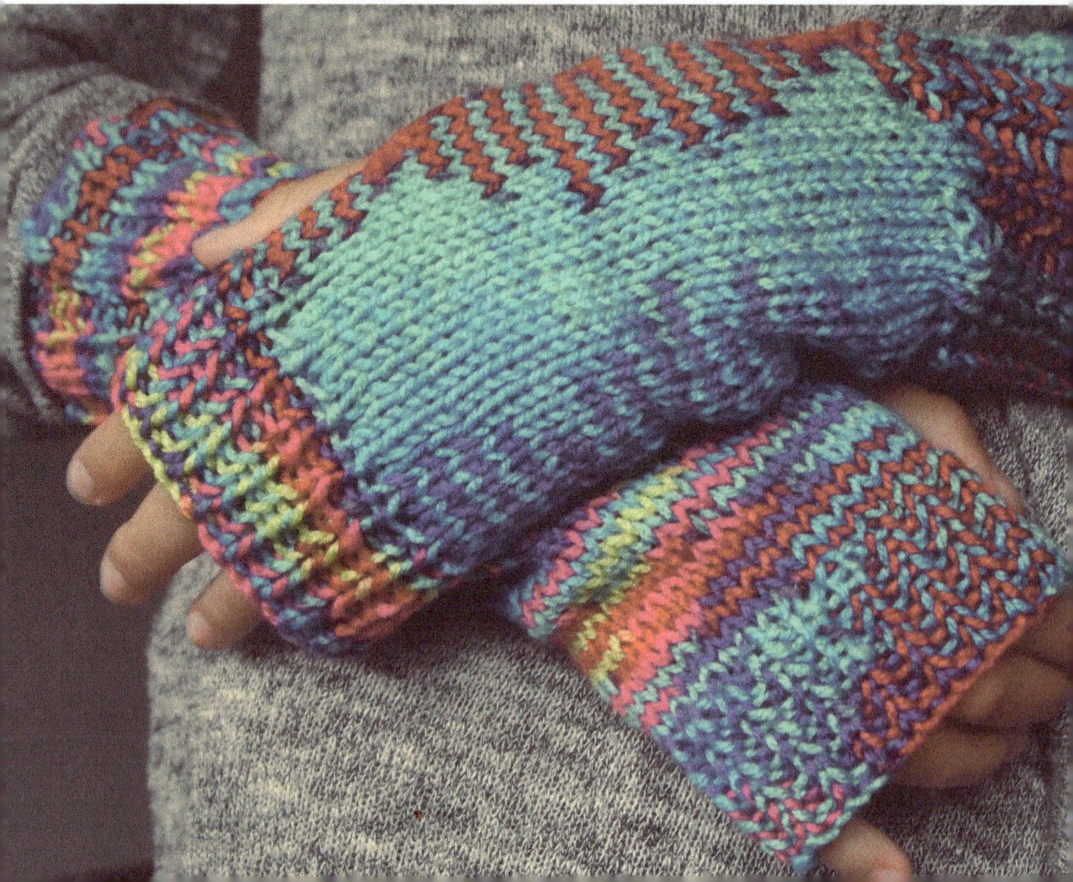

Once you see the old woman, look at the whole image again and try to shift back and forth between the two images—old woman and young woman. Notice your brain working to deconstruct the image you saw so easily. This is an ability that can be developed and improved. Working your mind like this is a way to develop flexible thinking. Life is easier with flexible thinking.

The meaning people make out of data is influenced by their experiences. We make meaning out of the data we get, whether it is experiential or factual.

Life is like this; even though we all see the same information and have similar experiences, we can also make very different meaning from what we see, which changes our experiences. This is about the uniqueness of people. Our actions stem from the meaning we have made about situations or circumstances with which we are presented. We can have different sensations for the same situations. It is possible for the sensations to change. Just like meanings can change, our feelings can change, and our brains can change.

2. Integrating Data

Integration is the result of combining separate things into an integrated whole. When the Logical Brain data is integrated with the Sensory Brain data, they form something completely new, something that did not exist before that can be used in a new way, creating more possibilities. For example, one can wear a sweater but not balls of yarn.

3. Synthesizing Data

Synthesis is the *process* of two or more entities coming together and forming a new entity, which is entirely different than any of the entities that make it up. The new entity transcends the ones it is made up of because it is in another state.

For example, the caterpillar is perfectly designed to crawl along the ground, trees, and other plants. To become a butterfly, the caterpillar must give up its way of being in the world and go into metamorphosis. During metamorphosis, parts of the caterpillar change and come together in a new way to turn into the butterfly. The butterfly has the same DNA but has a new and different way of being in the world. The butterfly's way of being in the world transcends the caterpillar's way of being in the world.

The World as I'd Known It Entirely Changed

Emelda came for therapy because she was struggling with issues in her marriage, specifically sexual issues. She had been married for less than a year.

In the sessions, her relationship with her parents came to the foreground. She told me that her parents separated when she was 11 years old. Her father moved in with their female neighbour, who lived down the street, and not long after that, her mother brought her new boyfriend into the home.

Emelda said her mother's new boyfriend molested her and that she was furious with her father for leaving the family. She said that if he hadn't moved out, she wouldn't have gotten molested. She had not spoken to her father in years.

During our work in therapy, she decided to reconnect with her father. When she did this, she got some new information. Her father had not wanted to move out, but her mother insisted, and he had not realized her mother was going to bring her boyfriend into the home. He told Emelda that he didn't know where to go. He wanted to be near her and her brothers, so when the neighbour down the street invited him to live with her, he accepted. He said it was not a love match.

This changed the meaning of her story completely. She felt betrayed by her mother and father for not explaining to her what each was going through and what happened. For her, it was as though the ground shifted underneath her and she felt shaken to her core. She had to let go of the old meaning she had lived her life by and develop a new sense of self.

Changing Meaning

Meaning can change by:

1. Adding More Information—Logical Data/Sensory Data

We rarely have all the information we need to make meaning, yet our brains are continually working to make meaning out of our existence by filling in the gaps. When we get more information, that is, more data—logical and/or sensory—the meaning often changes.

2. Changing the Context

Reframe the same information in a new way. Reframing means to frame or express information—words, concepts, plans—differently.

To reframe, you need to deconstruct the current meaning and reconstruct a new/different meaning.

Death/Rebirth

My client, Mandeep, had a sister who died before Christmas 2019. Mandeep had been struggling with the loss because she was estranged from everyone in her family. She said that she and her sister didn't get along when growing up but had reconnected as adults, making her feel less alone in the world. When her sister unexpectedly died, Mandeep felt alone again. She was so distraught that she couldn't work, so she went on medical leave. Not too long after that, because of her grief, she quit her job.

Mandeep turned to an aunt who had been good to her but felt her aunt's support was surface-level at best.

So, Mandeep reached out for therapy and was referred to me. Because she lived in Europe, we connected via videoconferencing.

I listened to Mandeep's story. She grew up in a family in which she felt invisible. From her experiences as a child, she developed a belief about herself—I don't matter; I only matter if I am pleasing others. She was always focused on others, not herself, trying to figure out what others wanted/needed and making it happen.

I told her that she had a mistaken belief, and I told her it was not true.

I then worked with her to change this belief. I developed a small ritual to deconstruct her original belief and then asked her to create her own belief. This started to shift how she felt about herself.

In therapy, I facilitated her expressing and processing her grief at the loss of her sister, her sense of abandonment, and utter aloneness in the world. I shared my story of loss with her and how it impacted me, which connected us. I sent her a bead bracelet to remind her to take a breath when she noticed it and to feel somewhat connected to me—halfway around the globe.

Her grief was deep and had gone on for a long time. She had disturbing dreams. I shared with her my experience of the time I died in a dream. I told her that dying in a dream can mean letting go of a part of yourself that you need to let go of—a part of you that you weren't born with but helped you survive childhood.

About a month later, I received the following email from Mandeep:

"I had a strange dream last night. I am a terrible sleeper and hardly dream. In it, my sister died, but then shortly after, my aunt and Gregory (her life coach) also died. The dream felt very sad, but it made me think of the dream you said you had about dying. I have been trying to do a lot of work on getting in tune with what I want rather than what other people have told me I want. I am beginning to explore career paths that once seemed crazy to me. I'm curious if the two are related. Maybe it signifies that I'm ready to step into my own."

I was pleased that she had taken in the information about death and dying in dreams. It helped her frame her experience in an emotionally healthy way, which she wouldn't have been able to do without this information.

I told her that the dream was positive. Death is about letting go, and her dream meant she was letting go of the significant people in her life. With Gregory, it meant she was letting go of him too because she no longer needed him in the same way. I told her that she had let go of needing others because she had reclaimed the young child within who had been frozen in time.

She had created new neural pathways and was ready to focus on her own life and passions.

3. Shifting Sensations

Our senses are constantly picking up data from the universe and sending it to our brains, whether we are awake/asleep, focused on a task or lounging on the swing on the back porch.

Most of the time, we are not aware of this accumulation of information. When we sleep, our brain goes into REM sleep, and all the data integrates and synthesizes it with what our Logical Brain has thought about, analyzed, and learned. Frequently, we get sensations that build up and break into our awareness.

Examples of shifting sensations:

The Relationship Ran Its Course

Tyrell, born in Trinidad, had lived in Canada for 21 years. He met his wife, Elizabeth, years ago when she was vacationing in Trinidad. He came from a large, low-income family. He and Elizabeth fell in love, and two years later, they were married and living in Canada. They both wanted a family and happily agreed that she would be the breadwinner and he would stay home with the children. This arrangement worked well for many years.

Things shifted when their children were in elementary school and Tyrell started dabbling in real estate. However, he didn't find much success in real estate but had always been passionate about music. Unfortunately, it was not lucrative, so he continued to ride Elizabeth's coattails throughout the marriage.

When their children reached their teenage years, their marriage went into a natural stage of reorganization. Since both Tyrell and Elizabeth realized that their children would leave home in a few years, they did what most couples do at this stage; they reassessed their spousal relationship.

So, Tyrell and Elizabeth came to therapy, and we identified their negative interactive cycle.* Elizabeth was tired of doing the emotional and financial heavy-lifting, and Tyrell was tired of being the nanny and running the household. As therapy progressed, it became evident that there was little goodwill left between them and even less love, and their resentment was palpable.

They decided to have a trial separation. Even though Tyrell didn't have a stable, adequate income, he decided it was in his and their children's best interests to move out. It was time for him to come into his own as an adult, man, and individual in his own right. He was apprehensive yet accepting of this personal growth.

*NOTE: Therapy Framework: EFT Emotionally Focused Therapy for Couples

Figure yourself out here.

The rest of their sessions focused on grieving the breakup of their family unit. I helped each process their emotions by guiding them to breathe through the sensations of grief and loss to the depths. As the intensity of the sensations lessened, each started to feel a sense of relief.

I told them that a trial separation is just that—a trial. Sometimes, couples need to completely let go of the way each had been in the marriage before there is any possibility of reconnecting in a new way. I told them that their old marriage was dead and needed to die. It was not working for either one of them, and it was no longer emotionally healthy for their children. I encouraged each to let the old marriage die without guilt or judgment—to shift sensations. I talked to them about the concept of death/rebirth. I told them that if they can come together again in a new way, they will create a new marriage that will likely last the rest of their lives.

Emotionally Frozen

Macklem, a 58-year-old married man, was referred to me by his doctor. He was deeply depressed, so depressed that he could barely talk.

Prior to his first marriage, he had been in a long-term relationship for 25 years with a woman 18 years his senior. Three years ago, he was blindsided by his common-law partner's sudden ending of the relationship. He didn't see it coming and was devastated. He described himself as "a ship that had lost anchor in the night and was being washed up on the rocks."

He immediately went online, quickly met a woman, and married her shortly afterwards. Now, three years later, he was deeply depressed. He described his current wife as "very nice and kind" and said he's been floating through their marriage the past three years.

Macklem was terrified of the relationship ending because he feared the sensations he experienced with his previous breakup. However, he didn't articulate it that way; he said he was terrified of being "left to float again." Once he started therapy, he felt relief at being able to tell someone his story.

I advised him not to make any decisions about his current relationship; his focus needed to be on his personal recovery.

I asked him to tell me about his childhood, and he said that his father was always angry and that his parents fought a lot. One memory stood out for him: He was 13-years-old and wanted to attend a concert with his friends. However, his father wouldn't let him, stating he was too young. Regardless, he snuck out and went with his friends anyway. When his father found out, he beat him badly, and it took him a long time to recover from the physical and emotional trauma.

I talked to him about how important puberty is and how a father's developmental task is to welcome their sons into manhood. I told him his father did the opposite. The beating traumatized him, leaving him frozen in time at age 13 (probably even younger). He resonated strongly with what I said.

I told him that our therapeutic work needed to revolve around helping him access and process the old wound and heal from it—he had been living in limbo because he was no longer a child yet had not come into his own as an adult. I also told him how he had no one who advocated for him throughout his life, so he couldn't learn to advocate for himself.

In therapy, I helped him facilitate his accessing and expressing the sensations of terror and alienation at being left afloat.

I typically give clients homeplay (not homework) to do between sessions. I suggested that he start taking classes in some attacking-type sport, such as boxing, wrestling, martial arts, etc., to get the skills to fight for himself and revise his mistaken belief to understand that he was worthy and worth fighting for.

He chose boxing and started feeling better about himself almost immediately, and it showed in the way he carried himself.

Macklem is still in his relationship; it is changing because he is changing. I advised him to let go of the outcome; time will tell if he and his wife can develop a new relationship or let go of this one because it has run its course. It will be his decision from a healed place.

Modus Operandi

Modus operandi is a consistent way/pattern of operating with the self, others, and the world in general. It is a person's "way of being" in the world. It begins at birth and is stabilized around five to six years of life. It may stay the same for a person's lifetime or be changed by the circumstances and conditions of a person's environment. It can also be changed by focusing on the modus operandi directly.

Babies are born with innate characteristics that stem from their genetics, energy levels (passive/active, fragility/hardiness), levels of curiosity, sensitivities, interests, urges, and the need to attach. We tend to think of babies as all the same. In many ways, they are. However, they adapt these characteristics from birth to meet their survival needs. Each baby is different in significant ways. How the mother (and other caregivers) interacts with the child impacts the child's emotional and physical development. What the child witnesses also affects their emotional and physical development.

From birth to age six, babies and children must figure out their bodies and how they work. They must figure out how to interact with others to best survive in their family, culture, and the world. Most of what they learn is by mimicking others, interacting with others (teaching, helping, guiding), and trial and error. Children tend to do more of what gives them pleasurable feelings/sensations and avoid what gives them unpleasant feelings/sensations.

By age seven, children have had millions of experiences. From all those experiences, they have figured out patterns and recurring events and adapted to them. Eventually, they developed an idiosyncratic (unique) way of being for living their lives. They have a sense of who they are, who others are, and how the world is. From this, they conclude how to be or not be, what to do or

Personal Story—Bea's Modus Operandi

When I was 36, my marriage went into a natural reorganization when my youngest child entered kindergarten. For seven years, my life had been focused on raising my babies and caring for our home. Our marriage needed to shift, and we needed to make changes, but we weren't handling it well. I found a therapist, and in talking with the therapist, I discovered my modus operandi.

I grew up on a farm which was often dangerous. I was the youngest of four in my family. My parents were hard-working. My siblings often had to look after me while my mom and dad worked. They were bigger, older, and more capable than I was.

I am…little and helpless. (I was emotionally developmentally arrested at an infant level)

Others are…smarter, more competent, more capable.

The world is…a dangerous place.

Therefore…I must always have someone to look after me.

Here I was at 36, acting like a little girl. I was certainly not little and helpless. I was successfully running a household and mothering two children. The world was a dangerous place, but it was certainly not THAT dangerous. I didn't need anyone to look after me, including my husband. However, I wanted a healthy grown-up relationship with him.

Therapy focused on helping me process the trauma I experienced in childhood.

not do to best survive, cope, and thrive. At this young age, they are inexperienced and ignorant of many factors. The conclusions they make may be accurate, partially accurate, or they may not be accurate at all. Often, they are not.

Humans tend to behave in ways that bring sensations of pleasure and satisfaction and are meaningful to them. They want to feel sensations of safety and security. They tend to behave in ways to avoid sensations that cause discomfort and pain and are meaningless. Most people do not want to feel sensations of risk, danger, and insecurity. Some people thrive on thrills and excitement constantly seeking it out.

Associations influence meaning. Many people go about their everyday lives unaware that they are avoiding sensations. People develop habits to avoid situations, circumstances, and people they associate with stressful and uncomfortable sensations they have felt in the past. Their intent is to manifest sensations that they like and enjoy.

However, people will also stay in situations they associate with danger because they are familiar and give the illusion of safety. For example, people will stay in abusive relationships because they occasionally experience moments of love and safety amongst the chaos and danger.

Children need to make sense of the world to survive. By the age of seven, children have created a modus operandi. They have made meaning out of their lives. This is how they operate in the world. They need to know they developed this mode, and it can be changed. Most people are convinced they are genetically programmed and cannot be changed. It is an adaptation to the world (family, culture, geographically/economically) they are born into.

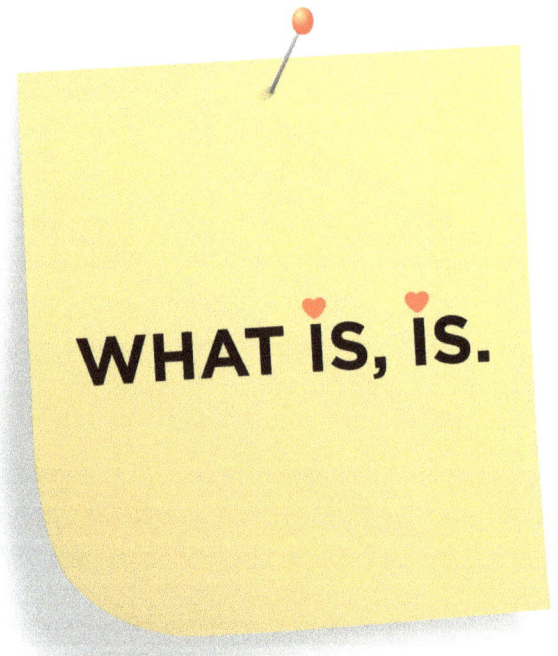

Depending on the events and circumstances, a person's modus operandi can be changed, but often it is not. Sometimes people do not think they can or know how to change it. A person's modus operandi may work well in childhood, but it does not work well in adulthood. While it may help us survive when we are children by serving as a coping mechanism, it can often keep us from thriving as adults.

A person's modus operandi becomes a pattern of their entrenched habits. Fortunately, habits can be changed. Even bad habits, such as drinking and smoking, can be changed. Therefore, a person's modus operandi can be changed. We can identify the strengths of our modus operandi and build on them, and we can identify the weaknesses, target them, and change them. People often say, "This is who I am" (stubborn, lazy, hard, etc.) as though they were born that way. Typically, they were not.

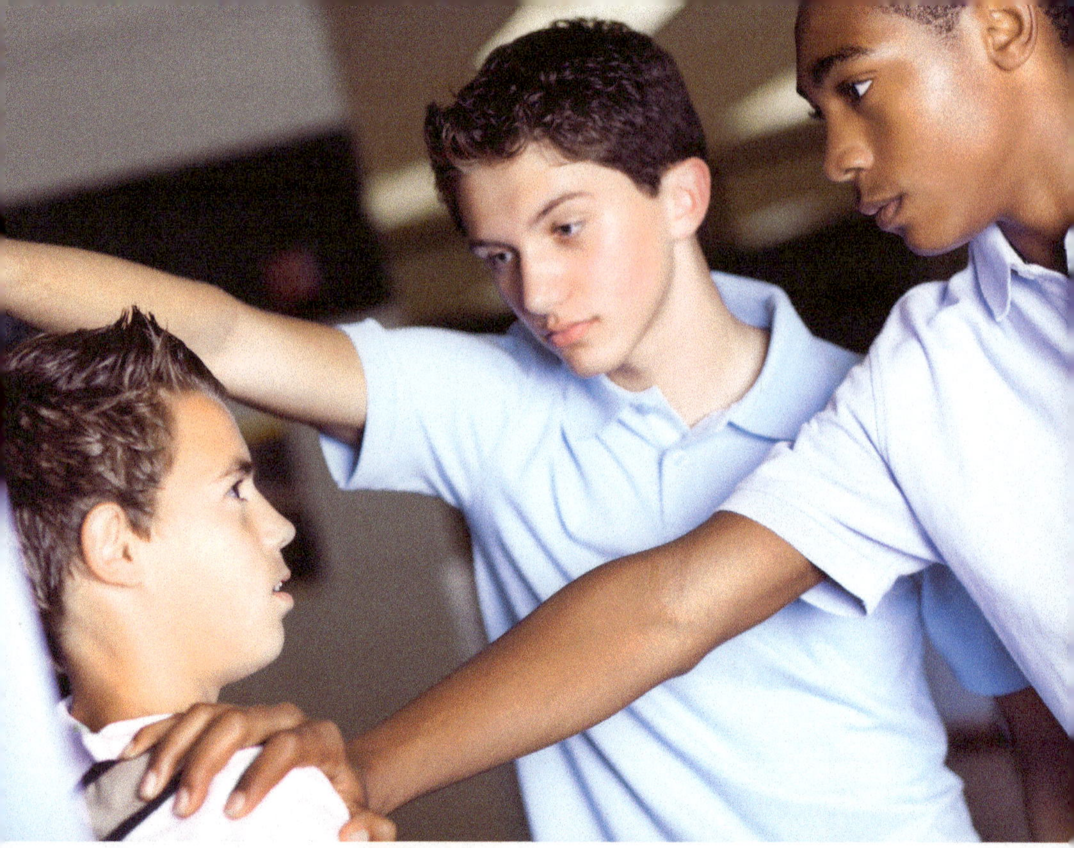
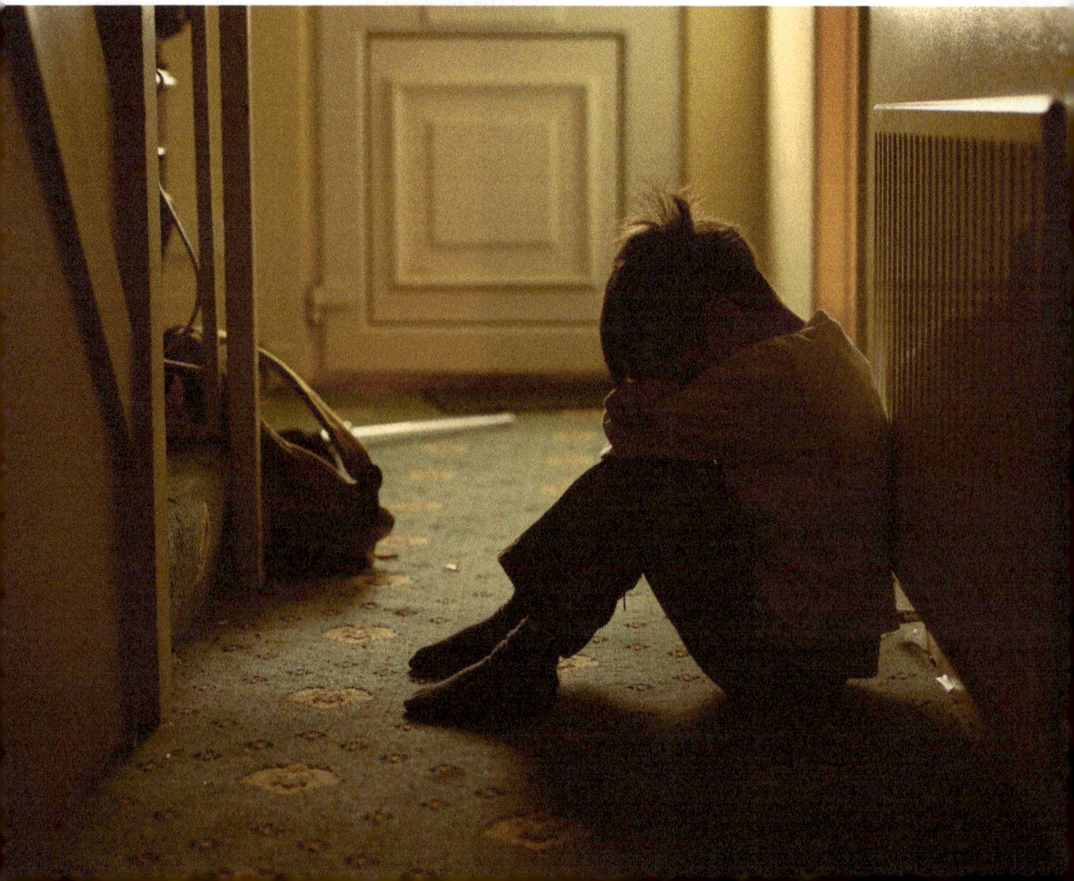

Transcending the Old Way

Gusto and Francesca had been seeing me for couples counselling for some time.

Gusto was a large man whose mother abandoned him when he was a child. Francesca was a petit woman who grew up with a father who beat her frequently. Each had not felt safe in their family of origin for different reasons.

In therapy, we identified the negative interactive pattern between them. Gusto would often get insecure when his wife would go out with her friends. His modus operandi was to avoid feelings of abandonment. Francesca was a runner and had some male and female friends with whom she ran. Often, she would be gone for 3-4 hours at a time when she went for a run. When Gusto felt the sensations of abandonment, he would cling to Francesca when she left or when she returned.

Francesca feared being dominated and controlled. Her modus operandi was to avoid being dominated. When Gusto clung to her, she would feel the sensations of being trapped, and she would pull away. When she pulled away, Gusto's abandonment issues would get triggered, and he would cling to her more. The more he would cling to her, the more controlled she would feel. They played this dynamic out in every aspect of their lives.

I worked with Gusto on processing his painful sensations of abandonment. I helped him access and breathe through the waves of intense sensations. When he was triggered, the sensations were so distressing that he would get desperate and believe that only hanging onto Francesca would stop them. He knew that this triggered her fear of being dominated, but he couldn't stop himself.

Similarly, I worked with Francesca to process the sensations of feeling trapped and dominated. I facilitated her breathing through the sensations and staying with them instead of trying to stop them. When she felt dominated, the sensations were so awful and intense that she just wanted them to stop, and she had to get away.

Several weeks later, they returned. They looked different and sounded different. They had a sense of calm within themselves and with each other. They had transcended the old dynamic.

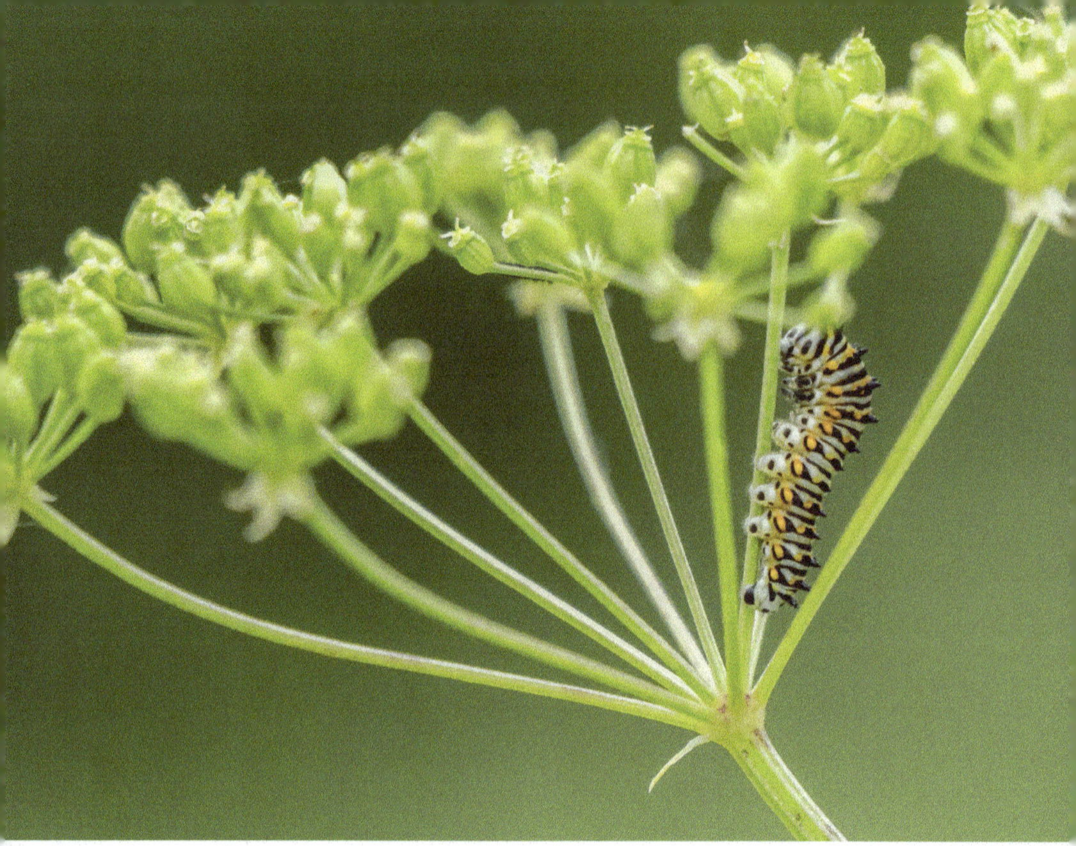

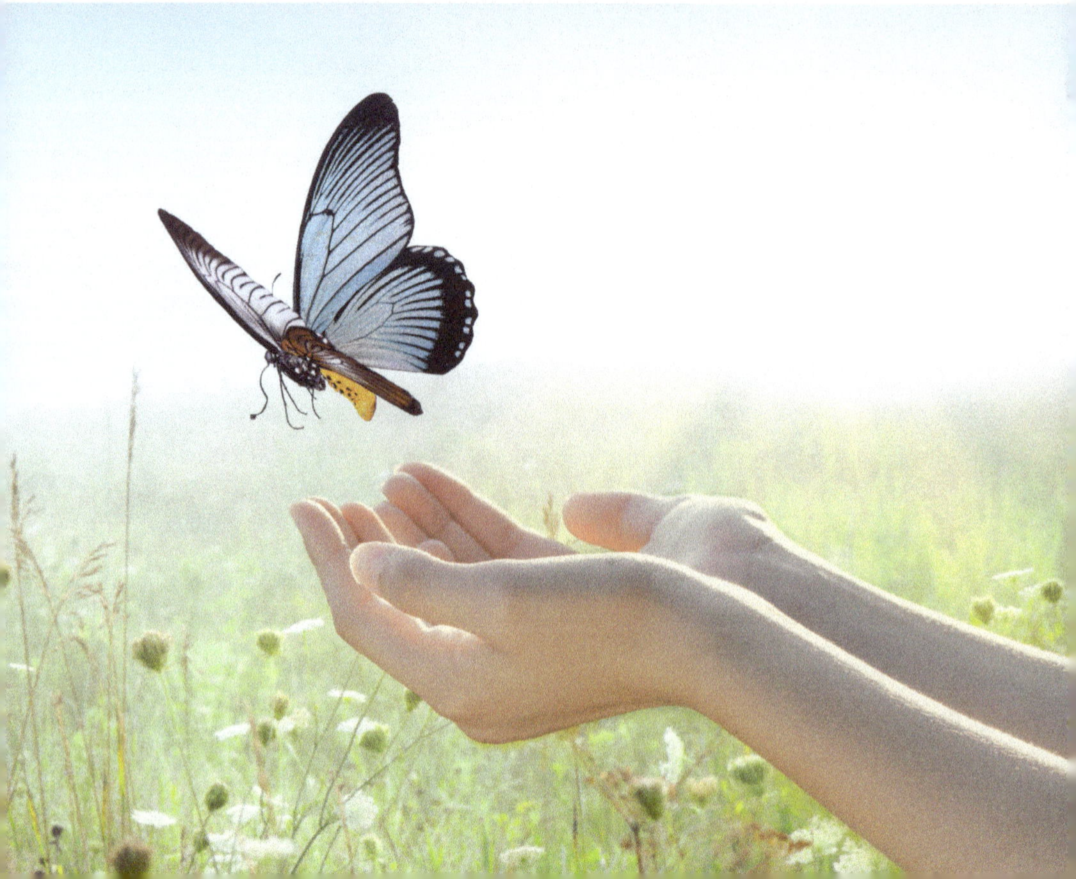

They told me they got into a physical altercation that escalated a week after our last session.

Gusto had pinned Francesca down, with his big hands gripping her wrists. He knew if he let her go, she would run out of the home, and his heart would break. Francesca was fighting for her life. She thought for sure she was going to die.

Then something happened. They don't know who did what first, but Gusto eased his grip seemingly at the same time as Francesca struggled less. At that moment, each felt loved and safe. Gusto said he knew that Francesca was fighting for her life, but the fact that she lessened her struggle meant she loved him. Similarly, Francesca said she knew Gusto was terrified she would abandon him forever, so when he loosened his grip on her wrists, she felt loved and safe. This shattered the tension between them, and they wrapped their arms around each other and cried with joy and relief.

They have a new relationship with each other that has a calm peace at the core. Now, when Francesca goes out, Gusto is not triggered, so he doesn't cling to her. When she comes back, she is loving and affectionate. She engages in more vigorous lovemaking because she is not afraid anymore, which Gusto loves because it reinforces his sense of connection with her.

Exercise

Identify your modus operandi by exploring your memories.

- They may be happy, fun, funny, and/or they may be sad, painful, scary.

- Take each one by itself and relive it as best you can.

- The memory is stored in the Sensory Brain, so allow yourself the time to access it.

- As you recall it, be aware of any sensations that are evoked.

- Breathe through the sensations.

- If you find a memory to be traumatic during this *process*, you might want to explore it with a professional. You may be recreating the trauma in your current life if it is not healed.

How to Help Others Help Themselves

Share your memories and dreams with others. However, choose wisely with whom to share them since you are sharing your unconscious way of operating in the world.

Key Takeaways:

- **Emotions impact meaning and meaning impacts emotions.**

- **Meaning is in the eye of the beholder and can change.**

- **Modus operandi is a person's "way of being" in the world.**

- **A person's modus operandi can change.**

CHAPTER SIX

Reshape and Liberate

"Things do not change; we change." —Henry Thoreau

Every time we learn something, our brain creates new neural pathways. An insight occurs when the brain creates a new neural connection, providing a new way to think about something or know something in a new way. This ability to change is termed plastic. The brain is very changeable. It is constantly adapting to increase a person's ability to function well no matter the circumstances. It can change a great deal in the short term and over the course of a person's life, meaning it is constantly changing from conception to a person's death.

Every time we have a new experience, our brain develops new neural pathways. When we have that experience again and again, we add to the neural pathway. To live life fully, we must (and can) change our brains (develop new neural pathways) so that we no longer need to *manage* but instead *process* and experience our *sensations*.

Deconstruction

If we understand how our brain makes meaning, we can "let go of" the meanings we have that are negative or wrong and then create new meanings. This is the concept of deconstruction—letting go of meanings we have made previously.

If we understand why and how people can look at the same stimuli and get different meanings, we know that meanings are not "etched in stone" and can be changed. Many people believe that the way they see things is absolute truth; therefore, they cannot be changed. This is called rigid thinking. Rigid thinking restricts understanding, blocks personal growth, and limits connection within oneself and with others. It also blocks the connection between the Logical Brain and the Sensory Brain, making it difficult to transcend old perceptions and generate new neural pathways. It keeps a person stuck in old problematic patterns of behaviour that generate the same old feelings with the same old sensations that are troublesome.

I am
not good
enough

I am okay
just as
I am

Flexible thinking allows for personal growth and connection within oneself and with others. The ability to "let go of" one's perception and allow one's brain to entertain a new view of the same data—logical and sensory—helps to create new neural pathways that transcend current neural pathways, precipitating new meaning, new sensations, and new emotions.

However, what has meaning for one person, can have a very different meaning for another. People need to understand that they can shift from rigid thinking to flexible thinking. They can start experimenting, keeping what works for them, and letting go of old habits/patterns that they no longer want to repeat, which helps them develop a healthier and more functional modus operandi.

Rigid mindsets have difficulty deconstructing (letting go of) the meaning they have made. Flexible mindsets do not. Deconstruction leads to creativity and newness and growth and excitement. Deconstruction is necessary to allow things to come together in a new way, which can lead to creativity and personal growth.

The most difficult part of deconstruction is letting go of a way of being that helped us survive childhood. Even if what we did in childhood hurts us in adulthood, we still do not want to let go of that way of being. It is like a kind of death, without knowing what our new self will be like.

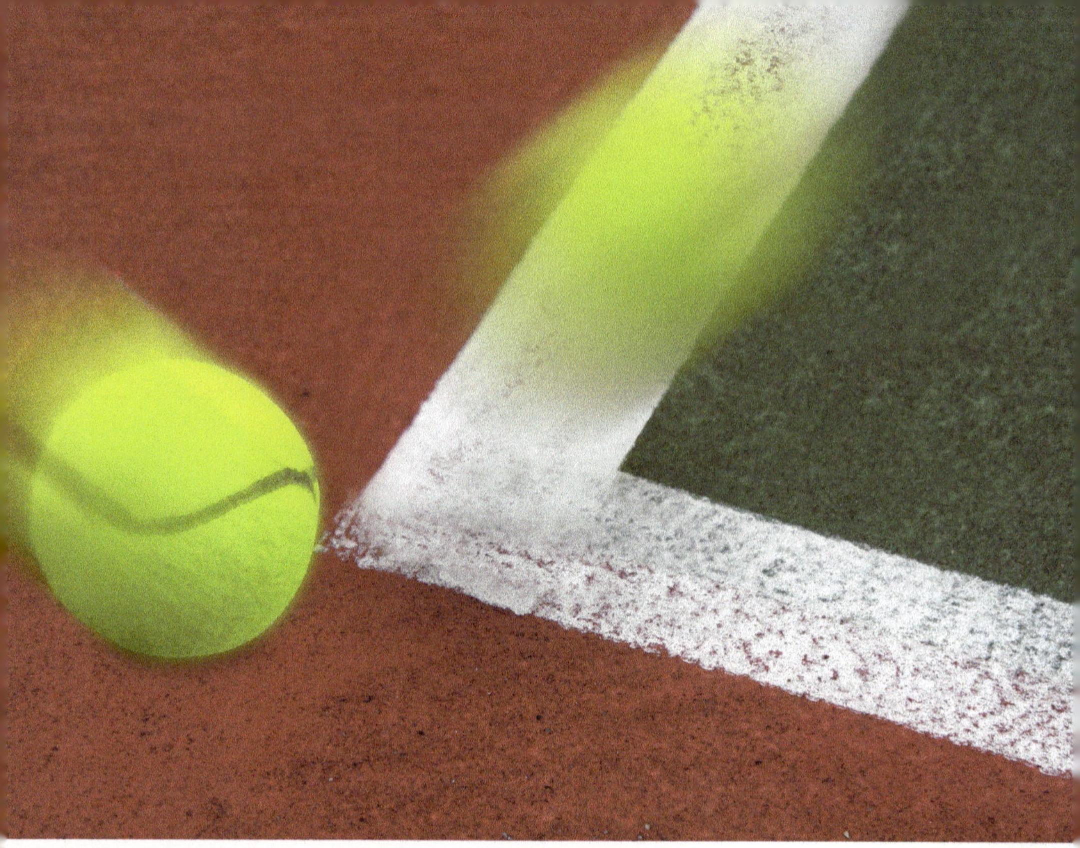

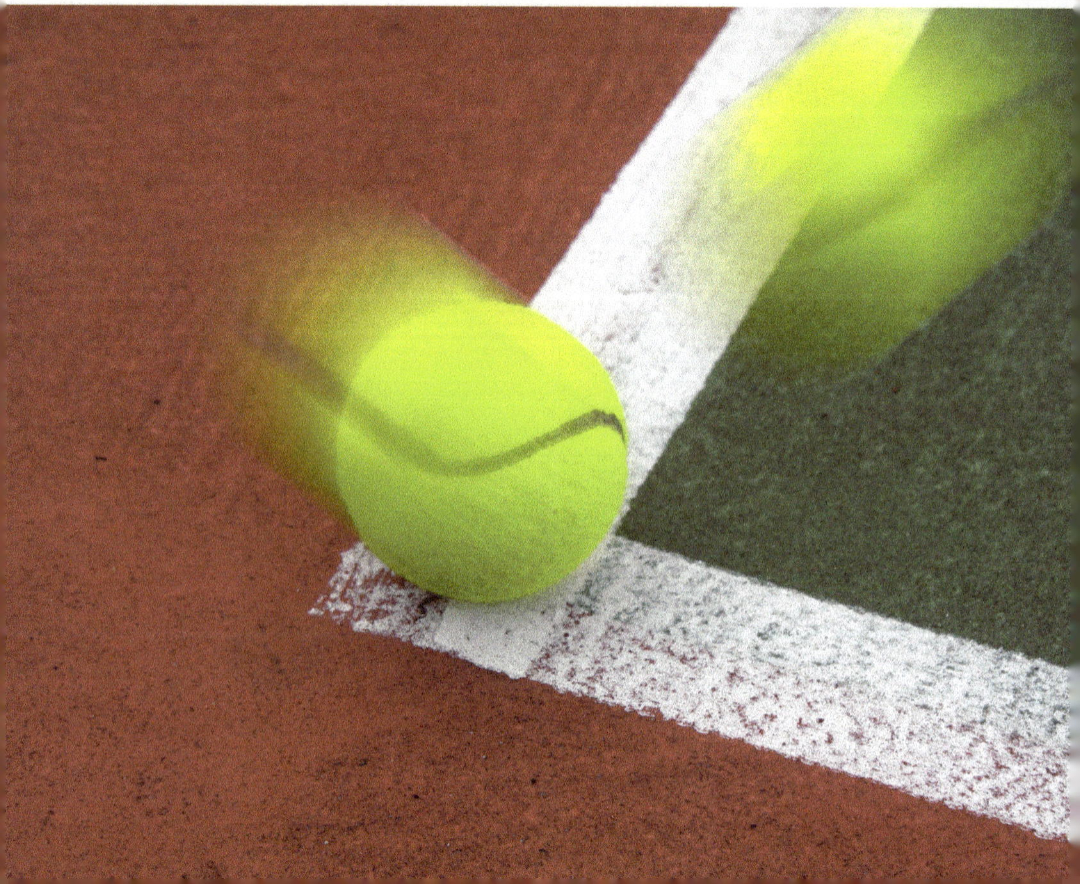

Personal Story—Seeing Is Believing

I learned a surprising life lesson while playing tennis. When playing recreational tennis, players call the ball "in" and "out" based on the rules of the game. Honesty is expected in fair play. However, sometimes, players call the ball "in" when it is "out" and "out" when it is "in." The rule is that depending on whose side of the court the ball lands on, that person makes the call.

I am very competitive when I play tennis. I can get very excited/worked up while playing, especially when I think my opponent is lying.

One day, my opponent returned the ball to my side. I watched the ball go toward the sideline. As I watched it, I saw it land "out." However, a split second later, I saw the ball land on the line.

I realized that I had visualized the ball landing out; I assume because I hoped it would land "out." The fact that my mind could do that so vividly made me realize that perhaps my perception is wrong sometimes; I want something or am afraid of something so strongly that my mind creates it. Or, maybe I have assumptions that I'm not aware of, and my mind operates on those assumptions without checking reality.

This experience convinced me that I may not always be right when I am sure I am. Having this experience changed how I view reality in all aspects of my life. Since then, I have been much more tolerant of myself and others.

THERE IS A RAINBOW OF COLORS BETWEEN BLACK & WHITE

People often jump to conclusions and act without checking things out or without seeking additional information to verify their perception of a situation. This can create problems.

People often know and are convinced that they are "right" about their views, feelings, actions, etc. Even when people are "right," what they do or how they do it does not work for them because others might not respond well. Let go of thinking in right/wrong, black/white terms. Rather than thinking in terms of right or wrong, ask different questions. For example, "Is this working for me?" "Is this working for others?" "Is this constructive?" "Is this destructive?" "Is this enhancing our relationship?" "Is this harming our relationship?" "Is what I intend to happen happening or not?"

When reasoning doesn't work, shift to strategies.

Please Don't Leave Me

Maya came to therapy for help with her relationship. She was happy with her husband, Tony, and their lives were going well. However, she was struggling with a problematic dynamic between them. She told me that he constantly complained despite everything going well. She said she had talked to him about it repeatedly, but he wouldn't change.

I asked her to give me an example. She told me that before he came home for dinner, she would make sure she was dressed attractively, the house was in order, and she would have a delicious meal prepared. She would always look forward to his coming home and them spending some time together. However, the moment he would walk into the kitchen, he would start complaining about something— anything. She would then feel hurt, resentful, and powerless to influence him, so she would pull back from him emotionally.

I told her there was nothing wrong with voicing her concerns with Tony if it worked. However, when reasoning doesn't work, one needs to shift to relationship-enhancing strategies.

So, I worked with her to develop a strategy to experiment with.

Step 1: Don't mention the topic/issue again.

Step 2: When Tony starts to complain, don't say anything. Instead, leave the kitchen and go to the bathroom. Take longer than usual. Then, return to the kitchen with a warm and friendly attitude.

Step 3: When Tony starts to complain again, don't say anything. Instead, calmly leave the kitchen, go to your bedroom, and change your clothes. Take a little longer than usual. Then, return to the kitchen with a warm and friendly attitude.

*Step 4: When Tony starts to complain again, calmly make an excuse to go to the store and **go**. Take as long as you want; visit family or a friend on your way home. When you return, have a warm and friendly attitude. If he is upset and/or angry, let him be angry. Don't apologize or explain.*

Keep repeating the strategy without explaining anything.

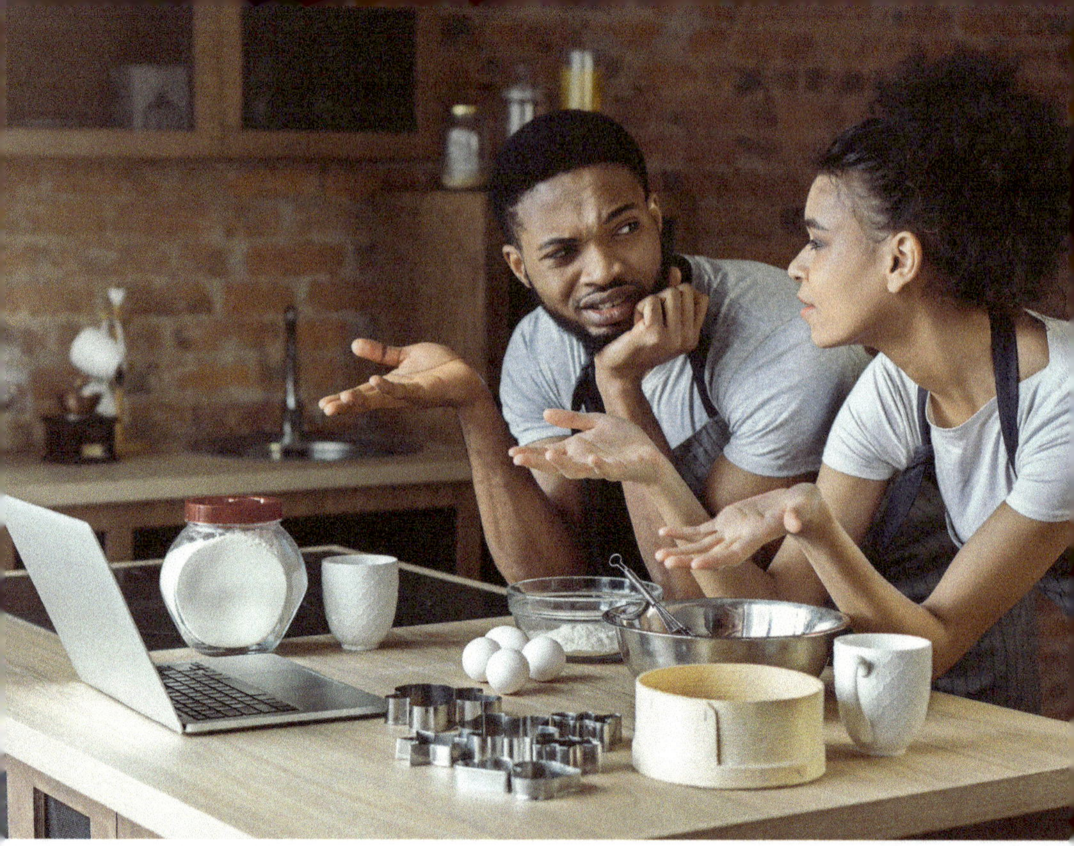

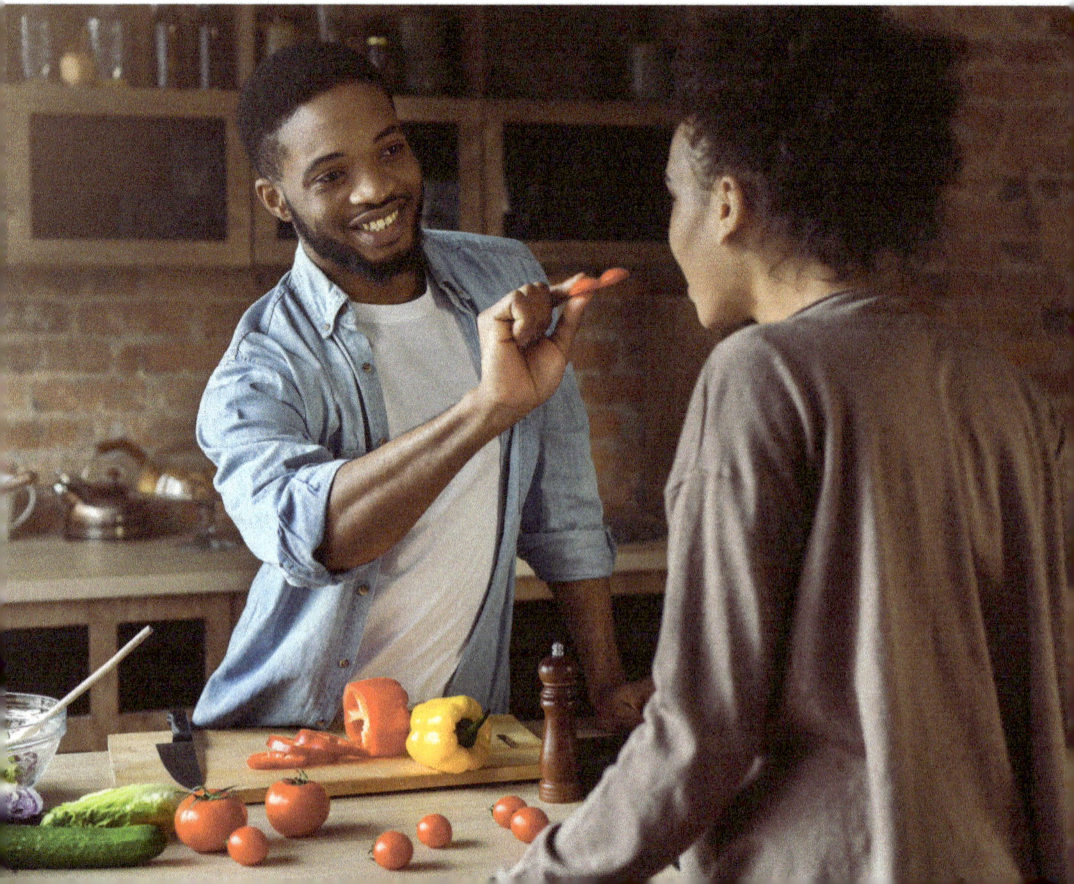

Maya came back for a session two weeks later and said that the strategy worked like a charm and Tony never even realized what was going on. This was puzzling to her.

I explained to Maya how and why the strategy works—it's all about the sensations.

Often, people don't have many experiences of emotional intimacy and closeness. In Maya's situation, she had more experiences of intimacy and closeness than her husband. When Tony walks into the kitchen and senses Maya's warmth, he gets sensations of discomfort, pressure, and expectation. When he starts complaining, which triggers Maya, Maya's warmth quickly cools, and she pulls away. When she pulls away and is not warm anymore, Tony's uncomfortable sensations go away, and he stops complaining. But the damage is done.

When people get uncomfortable, they go to their default neural pathways of pushing people away, just like Tony did when he shifted to complaining. Using my strategy, when Tony started to complain, Maya calmly withdraws her presence from him. Tony's uncomfortable sensations dissipated when Maya started withdrawing her presence (without a negative attitude). He didn't need to complain. He didn't want her to go away; he wanted to be with her. After a while, they started having good conversations and closeness. They were forming new neural pathways with every enjoyable moment together. The problem dissipated without "the talk," disparagement, conflict, or anyone feeling bad.

When one partner changes, the other usually responds to change with change of his/her own.

Exercise

How to stop thinking in black/white, right/wrong.

Shift from black/white, right/wrong thinking by asking different questions.

- Is what I am doing working for me and/or others?
- Is what I am doing: Constructive? Productive? Helpful? Healthy?
- Am I achieving what I intended?

If yes, do not change what you are doing.

If no, change what you are doing. If you do not know what to do, then:

- Experiment.
- Ask for advice from others.
- Ask others how they would handle your issue.
- Seek more information through the internet.
- Do nothing and observe what happens.
- Brainstorm ideas and solutions.

What is the impact of what I am doing/not doing on:

- Myself
- Other people
- My family
- My community
- My environment

How to Help Others Help Themselves

Help others create more neural pathways by exploring their fantasies:

Definition of fantasy:

- A fanciful mental image, typically one on which a person dwells at length or repeatedly and reflects their conscious or unconscious wishes.

- The faculty or activity of imagining things, especially things that are impossible or improbable.

Many people associate the term "fantasy" with sex. People fantasize about everything (not just sex). Fantasies can be in awareness and out of awareness. A fantasy can be partially in awareness and partially out of awareness.

This exercise is about helping a person access fantasies that are out of awareness.

The "What if…" game.

(NOTE: Play it as a game, not a therapeutic technique. Play is a Sensory Brain activity. Being playful and goofy together helps people connect and relate to one another.)

Example:

Dr. Bea: You've been talking about how bad your work situation is for several sessions now. You just said you should quit, and then you stopped talking. Let's explore what you think would happen if you quit. Are you okay doing this?

Client (hesitantly): Yeah.

Dr. Bea: You don't have to do it if you don't want to.

Client (engaged): Let's do it.

Dr. Bea: Okay. Finish this sentence: If I quit…

Client: If I quit, I won't have any money.

Dr. Bea: If I don't have any money, then…

Client: If I don't have any money, then I can't pay my rent.

Dr. Bea: If I can't pay my rent, then…

Client: If I can't pay my rent, then I'll have nowhere to go.

Dr. Bea: If I have nowhere to go…

Client: That's as far as I usually get. I usually see myself wandering the streets.

Dr. Bea: I'm going to ask you to go past this part. Let go of the facts. Let whatever pops into your mind come out.

Client: I'll be homeless, living on the streets (laughs). That will never happen. I have so many family and friends that I know I'll never be homeless.

The laughter is an indication of insight (creation of new neural pathways). The client recognizes that he could never be homeless. Once the client has an insight into his fantasy, he can explore it more. This buried part of the fantasy is now exposed; it is in his awareness, and he can address it and talk about it in a way he could never do before. For example, he may talk about how he would feel lost if he did not have his family and friends and how he is dependent on them.

It is an adjustment for people to know what they think unconsciously. When they say it out loud and hear themselves say it, they can take responsibility for it. When they take responsibility for it, they can believe it, or they can change it.

Often, fantasies end in death. Taking their fantasy to the ridiculous helps people revise their fantasies.

Fantasies that end in death also have the function of warning—be careful, you could get hurt or die. These fantasies are how people scare themselves to make them do something or stop them from doing something. This helps them live a more cautious life. The "What if…" game typically has a doom and gloom content and outcome.

Ask the person to play the "What if…" game with a positive ending.

Suggest they let go of logic, let go of reality, and let their mind go wherever it wants to.

For example: If I quit my job, I will get a better job.

The sillier and more fun it is, the more flexible their minds become.

For example: If I get a better job, I will make more money. If I make more money, I will be happier…

Just saying these statements out loud can positively impact a person's mindset, even if they do not believe what they are saying.

Experiment with different "What ifs…"

For example: What if you had permission to do what you wanted to do?

If I had permission to do what I wanted to do, I would stay in bed all day, quit my job, take a trip around the world, etc.

Key Takeaways:

- **The brain is always changing/ adapting/creating.**

- **Deconstruction (letting go of the familiar) is healthy.**

- **Rigid thinking keeps you stuck; flexible thinking facilitates personal growth.**

CHAPTER SEVEN

Give Up Control, Get Control

"One gains control by letting go." —Anonymous

Children are born knowing how to *process* emotions—by breathing through the waves of sensations as they experience them. As they do this, the sensations come and go until they are gone and there is nothing to *manage*. They grow and develop emotionally as well as physically.

Children first learn about expressing emotions in their families and culture. Some cultures are very expressive and comfortable with expression, while others are not. Children mimic others in all aspects of living. In some families, children will model the emotions of one parent and not the other. They may do the opposite of a parent they do not get along with or want to be like. Or, they model the expression of the more powerful parent or the passive parent.

Children learn to *manage* emotions indirectly through inter-actions with others, particularly parents and family members. Others who are not okay with expressing emotions may react by getting angry, being disapproving, showing disappointment, or by stonewalling, shaming, blaming, humiliating, and more. In the face of these consequences, children instinctively hold their breath and/or breathe shallow. When their emotions are not received well by their parents, they learn to block expression because of their need to be connected to their parents. Children who form strong attachment bonds with others are, specifically caregivers, more likely to feel a sense of belonging.

Children experiment with all kinds of behaviour until they find what works for them in their families. What works for them becomes a habit—a way of being in the world in the face of both negative and positive consequences. The habits they develop may or may not be emotionally healthy for them.

There are times when it is not convenient, appropriate, or possible to *process* emotions, so children learn to *manage* them. As they interact with others, they learn to interrupt *processing* by *managing*. Some may learn to *process* later when circumstances are favourable for expression (when it is safe to). However, many do not *process* later; they just learn to live with their *managed* emotions. That, too, becomes a habit—not an aspect of character.

Children also learn to *manage* emotions because they do not like to experience sensations that are uncomfortable, painful, too intense, frightening, or otherwise difficult. They *manage* because they do not like to feel the intensity of sensations. Most people do not like feeling the sensations of rejection, abandonment, sadness, or depression. A lot of people avoid conflict because they experience the sensations of others' emotions as intolerable. They might feel sensations that are unbearable and be afraid they will not be able to handle or survive them. The ultimate fear is that they might emotionally collapse, explode, implode, disintegrate or somehow, cease to exist.

Personal Story—Why Are We All Crying?

I was never a touchy-feely person; I never liked others touching me, nor did I like to touch others. In other words, I was not a warm person.

In my mid-thirties, I was in therapy. During a session, a memory came up that occasionally came to my awareness, but I never knew why or what it was about. I told my therapist: "I was three years old and remembered standing around the stove with my brother on one side of my mother and me on the other. My mother was making us popcorn, which in the 40s was a big treat. She would scrape the black kernels off the cob and put them in the pan, cover them with the lid, and then they would pop white. To me, it was magical. As we were watching the popcorn pop, I remember that both my brother and I and my mother were crying. Why were we all crying? This was supposed to be a special treat."

My therapy session ended around noon, but this memory wouldn't go away; it was like a hologram floating just above my forehead. I had the rest of the day to get through. I picked up my kids from school, made dinner, then put the kids to bed. All the while, I thought about this memory. Once I went to bed, I lay there awake, sensing the memory. I was not analyzing it. I was re-living it.

Around 4 a.m., I GOT IT!!. It all came together for me in what seemed like a "flash." We weren't all crying about the same thing. My brother and I were crying because our mother had just strapped us because she found us playing doctor and flipped out. My mother was crying because she felt remorse for what she had done to us. When I had that insight, I melted. Realizing she felt remorse made all my muscles relax, and forgiveness precipitated. I didn't think about forgiving her—forgiveness precipitated from the realization that she felt bad for what she had done to us.

The next day, I found myself spontaneously reaching out and touching others and liking when they touched me. I am naturally a warm person and have been ever since I processed that memory.

Powerlessness: Losing Control

Another sensation many people avoid is powerlessness. The worst sensations, along with hopelessness and helplessness, is powerlessness. Few can tolerate the experience of being powerless. Even animals hate feeling powerless. In our modern age, technology is creating distance between people. More and more jobs are lost to technology. As technology grows and becomes more pervasive, people are beginning to feel more powerless—they do not feel they matter or can make a difference. People start to feel insignificant.

The sensations of powerlessness are so awful that people do whatever they can to avoid them. One way to avoid the sensations of powerlessness is to shift into anger/rage. However, this does not make the powerless feeling/sensations go away. Instead, it numbs/masks the sensations of powerlessness. In this way, it feels less bad to feel angry than powerless. The rage, fueled by the engine of powerlessness, can sometimes be positive, such as when people make changes in their lives they were too afraid to make before. For example, someone quits their job and goes into business for themselves. However, typically, anger fueled by powerlessness is harmful to oneself and others. "Going postal" is an expression for people who feel powerless in their lives and erupt into violence or shift to cunningly planning strategic violence against others. When what they do gets attention, they prove to the world that they matter—in a destructive way.

Essentially, people do not like feeling out of control (unpleasant sensations), so they develop a set of behaviours that give them a sense of control (whether they have control is questionable). This becomes a modus operandi—a way of being—that may be healthy (both psychologically and physically) or unhealthy. This way of being in the world becomes so automatic that a person is no longer aware of it. They assume this is their basic character or nature, but it is not; it is just a habit.

Essentially, we attempt to control the outcome of events, trying to avoid *real* or *imagined* sensations that are uncomfortable and distressing. This could be as small as our cat turning up its nose at us or as big as getting rejected by a loved one. Imagined sensations are future-oriented. People imagine doing something or saying something and imagine the negative consequences. They never feel the sensations, yet they make decisions based on what they *imagine* the sensations would be.

The paradox is that the more you repress/deflect/minimize/block off the sensations, the more they build up and intensify. The more backlog of *unprocessed* sensations, the more difficult it is to *manage* them. Eventually, unless there is a significant change in one's habit of operating in the world, there is not enough personal energy to keep functioning in life. Eventually, a person's way of being in the world collapses; it takes so much energy to *manage* their emotions that they have nothing left to operate in the world, so their modus operandi breaks down. This is often referred to as a meltdown, midlife crisis, or burnout.

When people do not avoid the sensations of emotions, they live and strive for whatever goals/experiences have meaning for them. For example, writers submit their writing to publishers. When they get rejected, which is very common, they are affected by it, but it does not stop them from submitting their work again. Even though they are disappointed and sad, they can handle the sensations. Writers who avoid sensations of emotions imagine they might get rejected, so they never submit their writing. Jack Canfield wrote the first *Chicken Soup for the Soul*. Ninety-four publishers rejected it before a small publishing company accepted it.

KEY*

■ Terror

⟷ Extreme Disgust/ Repulsion

— Deep Saddness/ Grief/Loss

◎ Deep Shame

*More information about emotional sensations on page 62

Attempting to Be in Control by Avoiding Conflict

When people avoid emotions, they behave in a way they would not behave if they were not avoiding. If a person is afraid of the sensations of conflict, they are constantly trying to avoid the sensations and to do that, they do and say things that they do not want to do or say. In behaving this way, they create the conflict they are trying to avoid.

I Don't Want to Fight! / I Might Lose it!

My clients, Antonio and Maria, who had been coming for counselling for several months, experienced an incident that cut to the core of their relationship.

One Sunday morning, they were at the beach with their two young babies—a six-month-old and a two-year-old. The baby was in the stroller, and the toddler was nearby. A large dog came barreling toward them, knocked over the stroller, grabbed Maria's small leather bag and ran away with it. The dog owner chased after the dog and got the bag back. She handed the bag to Maria and offered to pay for the broken strap. Maria was in shock and sputtered, "It's okay," so the woman left. Antonio was so irate that he had walked away from the situation because he was afraid he might lose his temper and hurt the woman, expecting Maria to handle the situation. When they looked inside Maria's purse, they found that the dog had destroyed her phone with its teeth. Later, they saw the woman and her dog happily playing by the water, seemingly not at all distressed by what the dog had done.

They brought the situation to therapy. The issue was no longer the dog. Now they were distressed at each other for how each handled the situation.

Antonio was upset with Maria because she had not handled the situation well and said she always minimizes and deflects from situations that need addressing. He took no responsibility for his part in the dynamic between them.

Maria was no longer focused on what happened because Antonio was upset with her, and she was worried about how they would recover from the breach between them.

I focused on each of them and talked about how each needed to stop blaming the other and start taking responsibility for their part.

Both were terrified of conflict and avoided it in different ways. Antonio was so afraid of his own destructive impulses that he would implode. Maria would go into "freeze" mode and claim everything was okay. Her concern shifted from present to future, fearing how they would ever recover from this rift between them.

I asked each to book an individual appointment to address their own fear of conflict and then gave them a joint task to realign their energy.

I put it into an email so that they could refer to it afterwards when they were less upset:

"Antonio and Maria,

You are both highly allergic to conflict, but you react differently. It is time to act rather than react by taking action after the fact.

Let's use the incident as the impetus for change:

Maria—Remember that the hardest thing for you to do is exhibit behaviours that will help Antonio trust your judgment and have a positive impact on his anger. So, call the police and report the incident to them. This is practice for finding new/different behaviours to handle situations. When you meet with the police as a couple, ask them how best to handle the incident. This will prevent situations like this from becoming a marital issue and keep the anger/behaviours focused on what they should be focused on—the people/dogs who are putting others at risk and damaging their belongings.

Antonio—Remember that the hardest thing for you is not to get so angry that you need to withdraw yourself from the situation. To help Maria feel loved and safe with you, you need to express your anger in constructive and productive ways, i.e., chop wood or go to the gun range and allow your rage expression in that venue. You can do your part to keep the anger/rage focused where it should be instead of diverting it to Maria and having it manifest itself in marital issues.

Treat this as an exercise in handling emergencies and strengthening your relationship."

When people who cannot tolerate conflict get to their breaking point, they often act in extreme ways, such as act out, meltdown, or abruptly leave relationships. Or, they stay in an unsatisfactory relationship and get mentally and/or physically sick. Conflict occurs.

For example, when a person is afraid of the sensations of anger, they will overly accommodate or sacrifice their time, money, and energy. They often become resentful and angry, turning their anger back on themselves instead of the person/people they are angry with. They make themselves feel guilty, which fuels their habit of avoiding.

People who cannot handle angry sensations often develop a modus operandi of overly giving to others. Because it is so difficult for them to hold a personal boundary with others, they often attract people who take advantage of them. When they give to others, others tend to like it, and like them, so there is less chance of them getting angry.

The Hole in the Donut; She Had No Self

Minua came to see me for therapy and told me her story. Her husband had left her, complaining that she was too needy. She was 36 years old and had been married for 12 years. She claimed she had done everything for her husband. Whatever he wanted her to do or be, she tried her best to please him. She described the first years of their marriage as idyllic—they were inseparable and operated as one. Then things shifted, and the more she tried to be what he wanted, the more he complained about her the way she was. She gave up her friends and family. She worked at a job that paid her well but was not satisfying. She worked for the paycheck and focused on her marriage. Her whole life had revolved around her husband, and now she was lost. It was as if she'd lost her center; she was a failure. She did not know what to do with herself. She had no self; she had given it away.

Minua told me she had attempted to kill herself and had failed even at that. She believed she was worthless; she felt empty and had nothing to live for. She bought some hose and was going to make an attempt on her life. A neighbour noticed her with the hose and started talking to her. Minua burst out sobbing. Someone cared about her. Maybe, just maybe, she had some worth.

We started the process of reclaiming her "self."

Dynamic: Takers/Givers

Some people are givers, and some are takers. Takers love givers. Givers will promise to do or not do almost anything to avoid anger/conflict, so takers tend to get them to promise to do or not do things and then hold them to it when they do not. Givers tend to deny their feelings to themselves and others. They are not congruent; their words do not match their behaviours; they say they are happy, but they are not. People in their lives complain about this incongruency. Conflict occurs.

Feeding the Monster

Early in their marriage, Sal and Angelina were very happy. Sal was keen to do things for Angelina because he liked to make her happy. He was the giver in the relationship. Angelina adored Sal because he catered to her every need. She felt loved. She was the taker in the relationship.

With three children, a home, a dog, and a pair of canaries later, Sal was overwhelmed with the many things he had to do for his wife. This list was endless. He would do two things on the list, and then she would add four more. He started to procrastinate, which caused conflict. He would reluctantly agree to do things but then forget to do them. Conflict occurred. Sal started drinking, which numbed him. This caused conflict. He continued to make promises to do things that he didn't want to do because he didn't know how to avoid conflict. This caused more conflict, so Sal drank more because he didn't want to fight and argue. Sal eventually became an alcoholic. Finally, when the youngest entered school, they entered therapy.

Merry-Go-Round Fights

Couples frequently come to couples counselling discouraged and exasperated. They keep having the same fight over and over but never resolve it. I call these fights the merry-go-round fights. When an issue comes up, the couple hops on the merry-go-round and ride it until the carousel stops, and they get off.

After so many merry-go-round fights, one or both no longer want to engage when the same issue or any other issue comes up because they know they will go around and around in their usual way, and when it is over, nothing will be different. It takes energy to ride on the merry-go-round, and they no longer want to waste their time that way.

This kills the goodwill in a relationship. Each gets exasperated and tends to give up, and the relationship goes flat.

I work with couples to first identify the negative interactive cycle and then change how each handles their part. I encourage them to focus on their own change, not changing their partner. I help them shift from reactive to active. Then the couple can get back to a positive interactive cycle—working and collaborating on changing together. Goodwill flows again.

Dynamic: Active/Passive

Some people are active, and some are passive. They are attracted to each other in friendships, work relationships, and romantic relationships. This dynamic works well when the active person respects the boundaries of the passive person, and the passive person can hold their boundaries with the active person in a clear caring way. However, if the passive person is afraid of conflict and has trouble holding their own (boundary) with the active person, the dynamic becomes negative.

Passive people tend to detach from their feelings. They tend to suppress their anger and do not know they are angry. They tend to go along with whatever the active person says and does without communicating their views, likes/dislikes, opinions. Resentment builds up with each interaction, and one day, a minor interaction happens, and the passive person has an extreme reaction. The active person feels blindsided, usually reacting with, "Why didn't you say/do something?" "Why didn't you tell me?" "I thought everything was okay with us."

I Was Only Trying to Make Her Happy

Sally brought a reluctant Sid to couples counselling. She said that Sid had ended their relationship, and she had no idea why. She showed me a Valentine's Day card he'd given her two months previously that said: "You are the love of my life. Love forever, Sid." Sally was blindsided by the breakup.

"I didn't see it coming," she sobbed. "I thought everything was fine."

Sid acknowledged that he wasn't transparent with Sally. He said he didn't like conflict and would "go along" with Sally's wants and needs so that he wouldn't make her angry. He would go to restaurants he didn't enjoy, eat food he didn't like, watch movies he didn't like, and run errands and complete chores he didn't want to do because he couldn't say "no." His explanation for the Valentine's Day card was, "It was an important day, and I knew it would make her happy." However, after Valentine's Day, something shifted for Sid. "I started to forget to do things I had promised to do, and Sally got mad at me. I just knew I couldn't keep doing this, but I didn't know how to talk to her, so I just ended it on the phone. Sally asked me to come to counselling, and I couldn't say "no."

When he said this, Sally stared at him and said, "You could have talked to me."

He sat with his head down in silence.

Sid and Sally's relationship was over. Neither intended it to turn out the way it did. They were both good people trying to be a couple in the only way they knew how and with the communication skills they had. No one was right or wrong.

Sid grew up in a contentious family and hated conflict. Sally grew up in a family where her mother was in charge, and her father was mostly okay with it.

To start new was not an option for either of them. Sally said she could never trust what Sid said again, and Sid knew he would never be himself in the relationship.

I recommended that they each continue with therapy to avoid repeating this type of cycle in future relationships.

Emotionally Blocked People Try to Control

Emotionally blocked people do not *process* because they are afraid of the sensations of any emotions, whether they are positive or negative (pleasant/unpleasant, calm/agitated). Most people tend to avoid bad experiences. No one wants to experience painful and difficult feelings if they can help it. It is common for people to avoid any situations where they will feel or imagine they will feel awful feelings, specifically the sensations of their feelings. Without even realizing it, they become invested in avoiding. They try to control the outcome, and by doing so, they act in ways that limit their abilities.

Depression is mostly a symptom of an underlying real and/or imaginary block in a person's way of being in life. It is a symptom that there is something wrong in a person's life, and they believe they cannot change it, i.e., they feel out of control. They do not know what to do, so they maintain the status quo to not lose control. As a result, they get depressed. The person's internal energy is split and working against the self. The more personal energy that is busy battling itself, the less personal energy available to operate in the world. People who are depressed say they have no energy. What they do not realize is that they have a lot of energy, but it is pitted against itself, so there is little available to live life in the way they want. This is because people are uninformed about how their brains work and, therefore, are afraid to make changes. They just do not know what else to do.

Often, people do not know to breathe through a feeling of uncomfortable sensations, and they become overwhelmed until they disconnect from their bodies. As a wave of emotions emerges, this sensation creates more fear, and they hold their breath to the point the wave (sensations) cannot crest. As a result, they feel horrible.

Emotionally Constipated

I worked with Horatio, a 50-year-old man who was as a middle manager at a publishing office. When he came to see me, he had been on disability for depression for nine months with no sign of improvement. He hated his job but felt he couldn't quit for financial reasons and was too depressed to find another one. He said, "Every day, I would put on my monkey suit and go into the office. Then one day, I just couldn't put on the monkey suit anymore, and I have been off work ever since."

Horatio's energy was split. A part of him hated his job and wanted to quit, but another part of him wouldn't let him. This required a lot of energy, which made him tired and depressed. Ultimately, he collapsed, and the part of him that was pushing him to go to work could no longer make him go.

I worked with him to realign his energy. Over several months, I worked to allow each part of him to have expression. I detected repressed rage in his depressed state. He said he didn't feel angry. I told him that I believed he didn't feel anger/rage because he had been repressing it for so long. I told him he needed to channel the rage out of his body to realign his energy. I gave him a task to do at home. I told him to roll up a newspaper, wrap tape around it, and find something to hit.

When he came back, his demeanour had changed. He said he made five newspaper rolls with duct tape. He wailed on the pole in his basement until all the rolls were in shreds, and he was lying on them in an exhausted heap. He said he didn't feel anything at first, but as he continued, he accessed his rage and expressed it by hitting the pole. He said he got a huge sense of release and felt energized for the first time in years.

The rest of his therapy focused on facilitating his accessing of other emotions and learning how to process them. This helped him figure out what he wanted to do for work.

Several weeks later, he cancelled his session because he had a job interview, and I never saw him again.

Personal Story—If I Can Survive Losing My Kids, I Can Survive Anything

When my kids came along, I loved them so much. I thought, "If anything happens to them, I won't survive it." Because I was afraid of the immensity of the imagined feelings/sensations, I was uptight with the boys. They were healthy, active, rambunctious, playful, and curious boys. It made for many clashes between us because I was so fearful of them getting hurt—or worse. What I didn't realize was that in trying to avoid emotional pain, I was behaving in a tense and agitated way. I am sure it made them more active and reactive to me.

When my boys were 8 and 10, I went to the funeral of my good friend's 16-year-old son. A drunk driver hit him as he was crossing the road to meet his girlfriend at the bus stop. It was an incredibly sad event. The boy's uncle gave the eulogy. He said many things, which I don't remember, but I was struck by one thing. He said, "We only had him for a short time, but we wouldn't have not wanted to have that time with him."

This resonated strongly with me. If I lost my boys at the ages of 8 and 10, it would be tragic and devastating, but I wouldn't have not wanted to not have that time with them. I knew (emotionally) and realized (intellectually) that I could survive the loss of them.

Knowing I could survive the worst if it happened, I relaxed about the boys and their activities. That doesn't mean it was easy. However, I could enjoy them more, and they could enjoy life more. Our relationship thrived.

Emotionally Unblocked People Let Go of Control

Emotionally unblocked people *process*. People who *process* their emotions are not afraid of the sensations of any emotions, whether they are positive or negative (pleasant/unpleasant, calm/agitated). They know they can handle whatever sensations they experience. Because they *process* their feelings on an ongoing basis, the sensations never build up to unbearable levels. They do not need to control the outcome because they are not avoiding anything. All their energy is aligned and available to deal with whatever life hands them. They can focus on their wants and needs and do what they do best. Things tend to fall together in ways that could never happen if they were trying to avoid sensations—trying to control them.

Exercise

In therapy, I hear the metaphor, "I feel like I'm in a deep hole, and I can't get out of it. I keep climbing up, but before I get to the top, I lose my footing and fall back down," or "I do get to the top, and someone or something pushes me back in."

I tell my clients that they are doing the same thing repeatedly, hoping for a different outcome. They need to go down to the bottom of the deep hole and process all the unpleasant and intense sensations. At the bottom, they will find the secret passage and an easy way out to freedom and light.

Finding the Secret Passage:

- When you find yourself in a difficult situation that you think you have no control over, realize that what you are doing is not working, so stop doing it.

- The answer is to *process* the real and imagined emotions evoked when you try to extricate yourself from the situation/circumstances.

- You *process* by facing and embracing the sensations of the emotions you are experiencing and breathe through them.

- The sensations come in waves.

- Breathe through the waves of sensations until they are gone.

- By doing so, you will develop new neural pathways, which help you heal and evolve. They open possibilities that were not possible before.

- *Processing* the emotions will take you to the bottom of the deep hole (the situation you are trying to get out of), and you will find the secret passage out. This passage is easy to climb and takes you to a new and different place, one that is healthy, constructive, and productive. You are no longer stuck. In fact, being stuck is a non-issue for you, now that you are engaged and moving forward in your life.

How to Help Others Help Themselves

Help others identify their pattern of avoidance by asking them questions about their experience.

(NOTE: The questions should not involve any content.)

For example:

- Tell me about the last time it happened?

- What prevents you from getting out?

- When you think about getting out of the situation, what is the worst part about it for you?

- What do you imagine once you are out? What would that be like for you?

Key Takeaways:

- **By trying to avoid unpleasant sensations, we intensify them.**

- **The sense of control we feel when we try to *manage* emotions is an illusion.**

- **To become who we are fully, we must give up a way of being that has helped us survive childhood.**

- **Once we *process* the emotions/sensations, control is a non-issue; It just is.**

CHAPTER EIGHT

Heal the Trauma, Heal Yourself

"Your pain is the breaking of the shell that encloses your under-standing. Even as the stone of the fruit must break, that its heart may stand in the sun, so must you know pain." —Kahlil Gibran

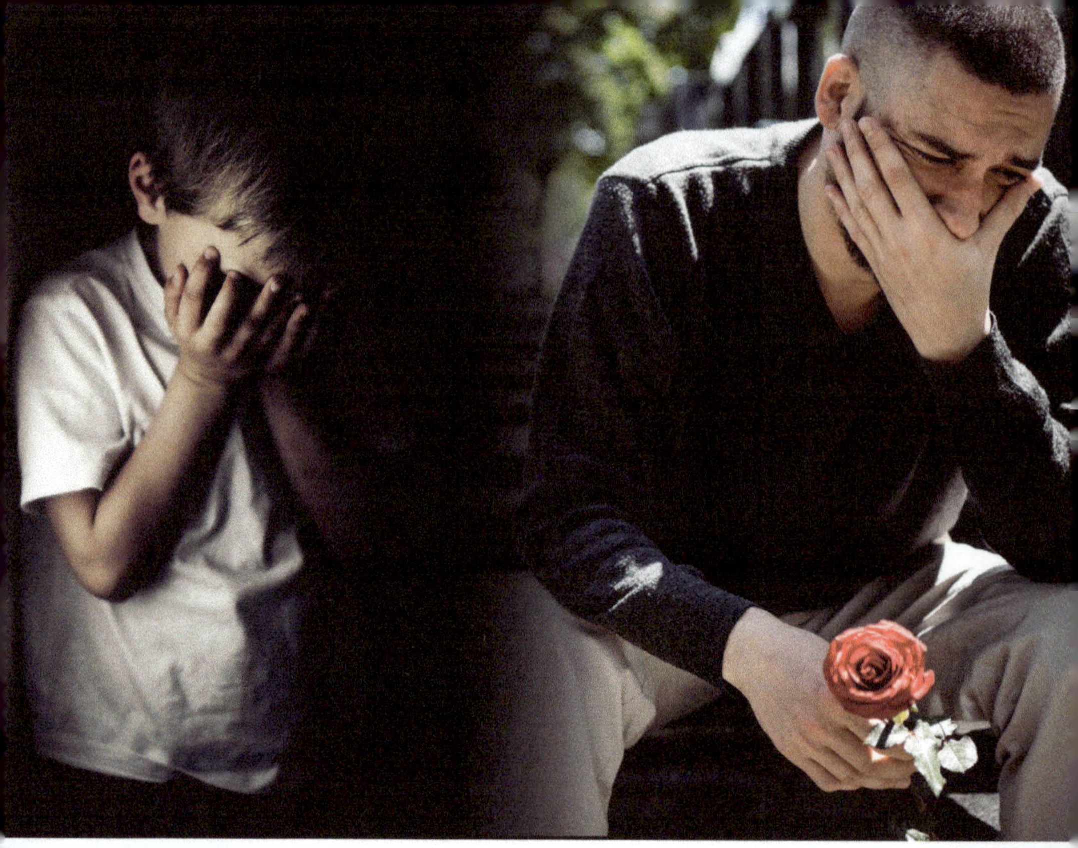
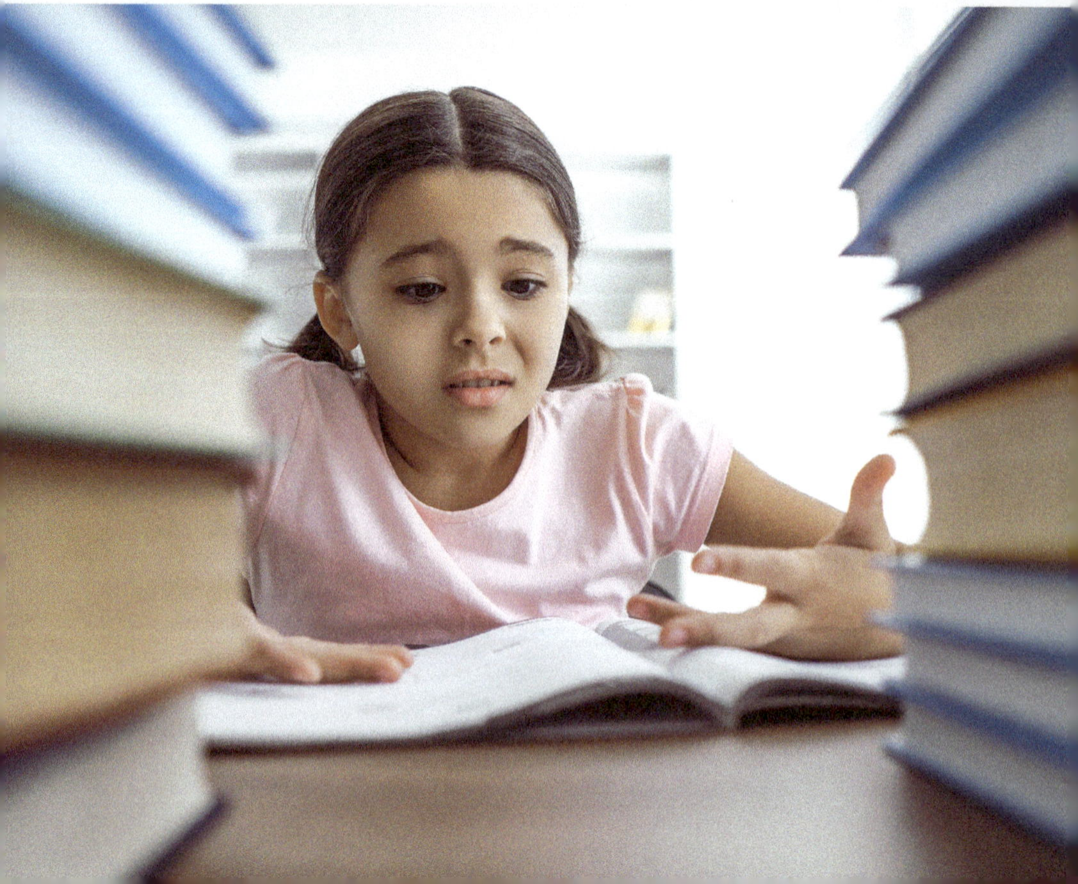

What is trauma?

Dictionary.com
> noun, plural traumas, traumata [trou-muh-tuh, traw-]

1. Pathology.

- a body wound or shock produced by sudden physical injury, as from violence or accident.
- the condition produced by this; traumatism.

2. Psychiatry.

- an experience that produces psychological injury or pain.
- the psychological injury so caused.

My definition:

Trauma is a difficult event that people experience/witness either physically or emotionally or a combination of both.
    Traumas can range from tiny to humongous, such as a stubbed toe to a near-fatal accident, a small disappointment to a major disappointment, a minor betrayal to a major betrayal, etc.

There are two styles of trauma:

1. Event trauma is a one-time event that has a negative, stressful significance for a person, such as a car accident or funeral.
2. Cumulative trauma (I call it the Drip Drip Drip Trauma) occurs during childhood, such as a child constantly being told they are stupid.

Event Trauma
One Time Doesn't Mean All the Time

Sigge remembered:

"When I was six years old, my family moved from a small rural town to a large city. On my first day of school, my brother walked me to school and left me as soon as we entered the school grounds. I spent the entire day scared because I didn't know how to get home. After school, I sat on the front steps, waiting, terrified no one was going to show up. I don't remember getting home or how I got home."

Modus Operandi:

Self: *I am on my own. I'm invisible.*

Others: *Others don't see me. They care about themselves.*

Life: *Life is overwhelming and scary.*

Therefore: I am on my own. No one cares for me, so I must figure things out for myself, or I will be lost.

In therapy, we explored this memory in depth. I helped her access the old terror in each part of the memory. As we explored it, she reclaimed more bits of information. She remembered that her teacher shared her lunch with her and spent time with her. She remembered sensations of discomfort when the teacher paid attention to her and shared her food with her. That was a new experience for her; she didn't know how to behave and felt many sensations of awkwardness. She remembered her brother coming to find her and take her home. He'd gone home, and his mother told him to go back to get her. She accessed sensations of relief when she saw him.

I guided her to re-enact the memory—first, how she remembered it happening, then as her brother and again as her teacher.

Then we "played" with the memory, having it turn out with a positive outcome and positive sensations.

At the end of therapy:

Modus Operandi:

> **Self:** *I am mostly on my own. I am sometimes visible and sometimes invisible. I am okay.*

> **Others:** *Others care about themselves, but some see me, help me, and share with me.*

> **Life:** *Life is confusing; there is a lot to figure out.*

> **Therefore:** *I am not on my own. I need to look for others to help me and be with me. I don't need to figure it out all by myself. I can ask questions.*

CUMULATIVE TRAUMA
I Wasn't Born This Way

Sam remembered:

"For most of my childhood, I was told I was clumsy. Both my parents told me I was clumsy, especially my mother. When I set the table for dinner, I would drop the dishes. When my dad tried to teach me how to ride a bike, I would fall off. My little sister could ride sooner than me. I remember trying hard not to be clumsy, but then I got worse. I couldn't figure out how not to be clumsy. It affected everything I did. Now, I have a motorcycle, and I can ride it, but I am riding it illegally because I know I will fail the driver's test."

Modus Operandi:

Self: I am clumsy. I am not as good as others.

Others: Others are better than me, more capable, and competent. They judge me.

Life: Life is complicated and tough to figure out. Life is serious business.

Therefore: I need to be careful all the time. I need to hide my clumsiness as best as I can. I can't have fun because I will mess up.

Sam didn't come to therapy to get help with his clumsiness. However, the mistaken belief that he was clumsy was a theme throughout his entire life. He couldn't relax and have fun.

In therapy, we focused on his mistaken belief, and I guided him through the ritual of destroying/deconstructing it.

I had him write on a large piece of paper: I am clumsy. I then asked him to date it and sign it. I explained that he was not born clumsy—that his experiences shaped him into being clumsy. I then asked him if he was ready to let go of this mistaken belief. I told him if he was not sure he should say so, and not rip if up until he was fully ready to let it go. When he was ready, I told him to rip up the paper and supplied him with a disposable garbage bag to put the shreds of paper in. Then I said, "Take this home, and make a small ritual out of destroying it and letting it go— either burn it in the fireplace, bury it in the backyard, or put it into a shredder if you have one."

Many months later, as we continued to work, I noticed he was doing things without thinking about them. He even stopped mentioning clumsiness. He got his motorcycle licence and was driving legally, so he enjoyed riding even more. He was taking racing courses and doing well in them. His friends started looking to him for guidance.

At one point, after he told me something he did that was adept and competent, I asked him, "Do you remember that you used to believe you were clumsy? He looked at me dumbfounded. He said, "I have completely forgotten about that." We celebrated his success with a high-five. I thought it was important that he acknowledge he had healed.

Modus Operandi:

> **Self:** I am capable, athletic, and adept. I can heal myself.

> **Others:** Are okay. Most are good, and many look to me for advice and guidance.

> **Life:** Life is dangerous, but it is also fun and interesting. Life is good.

> **Therefore:** I can do what I want and how I want. I am no longer concerned about how others judge me.

Perception and Trauma

A bad experience for one person may be funny or enjoyable to another. An emotionally moving experience for one person may be neutral to another.

Same Event, Different Experience

George and Gregory, twin brothers, age 35, were in therapy simultaneously but with different therapists. Unbeknownst to the other, each told the same memory.

George recalled:

When we were ten years old, my twin brother and I went to a friend's birthday party. When it came time for the cake, our friend's mom told us to sit at the dining room table. She then went into the kitchen, put the candles on the cake, and lit them. As she carried the cake into the dining room, she tripped and dropped the cake. It went all over the floor. We all immediately dropped to the floor and started eating the cake off the floor. It was hilarious!

Gregory recalled the same story but with a different ending:

…As she carried the cake into the dining room, she tripped and dropped the cake. It went all over the floor. I watched the kids dive onto the floor and grab handfuls of cake. It was disgusting! I was shocked. I sat frozen on my chair and just watched.

Both brothers recalled the same event. Why did one experience it as funny and the other as disgusting?

One fact about twins is that they tend to polarize. For example, the easy child/difficult child, the extrovert/the introvert. Therefore, this is a factor that can help explain the difference. However, why did George experience it as funny, while Gregory experienced it as disgusting? Why wasn't it the other way around?

To me, this is the mystery of people. We can often guess what others are experiencing, and our assessment can be accurate most of the time. However, these are usually just assumptions.

Often, when I listen to clients, they do not know what they feel, what they think, what they sense, or even how they act. I will reflect back to them what they are telling me or showing me with their verbal and non-verbal cues/behaviours.

I try not to assume, so when I find myself assuming, I check out my assumptions.

Example 1: What are you experiencing? Positive, negative, or neutral?

Example 2: What happens to you when you hear that? Pleasant, unpleasant or neutral?

Example 3: You seem relieved. Does this ring true?

Reflecting my clients' thoughts, feelings, and non-verbal changes in their body back to them helps them figure out what they think/believe, what they are experiencing, and how they behave. Many people will react to what they say with: "I can't believe I just said that!" "I didn't know I felt this way!" "I am surprised to know I think that!"

I'm Fine! I'm Not Tired!

Jon, a businessman, age 42, came to therapy to talk about a breakup he had gone through a couple of months earlier. As he spoke, I noticed he was tired physically and emotionally. I listened and then reflected back to him what he was telling me.

Bea: You sound kind of tired.

Jon: No, I'm not tired.

Bea: You sound tired.

Jon: Not really, I'm concerned about... (talked about his concerns)

Bea: I believe you when you say you don't feel tired. You just sound tired to me.

Jon: No, no. I've been really busy with... (mentioned what he was busy with)

Bea: That sounds exhausting.

Jon: That's the nature of my business...

Bea: Tell me again about that.

Jon: (talked about it some more)

Bea: I feel exhausted just listening to what you've gone through in the last six months.

Jon: (long pause)

Bea: (waiting in silence)

Jon: (in a slow, tired voice) I just realized how exhausted I am.

Bea: Allow yourself to feel the fatigue you've been blocking off. Take your time.

Jon: (silence)

Bea: (soft tone) Stay with the sensations of fatigue and breathe. Sensations come in waves, so allow the waves to crest and fall.

Jon: (silence)

Bea: (soft tone) Breathe into every tired cell of your body. Now, you can rest. This is important.

It took Jon a long time to connect with his body. When he finally did, he could feel the sensations of fatigue. Then he knew he was exhausted and could acknowledge it.

Trauma from Experiencing

People often get traumatized by seeing or witnessing events or situations that are sad, horrific, catastrophic, etc. Soldiers in war see and witness many frightening situations and cannot get the images or sounds out of their minds. Doctors, nurses, paramedics, and firefighters also witness gruesome situations. People can be traumatized by the news, such as watching the attack on the World Trade Center with people leaping to their deaths.

People who witness trauma will often minimize it. They will say, "Nothing happened to me." Often, people who witness events do not even know they are traumatized.

Blindsiding

Being blindsided is a trauma in and of itself, and what happens as a result of being blindsided is also a trauma. Often, people receive treatment for the second trauma, but not the blindsiding.

When someone is blindsided, they cannot perceive the truth of a situation. They have been caught off guard by either seeing something they did not expect to see, by having an accident, being attacked, being sexually abused, or learning new and shattering information. It could also be a combination of the above.

What happens is that a person's understanding of the world and how it works becomes discombobulated. Their modus operandi has been destroyed, and they must now figure out a new way of being given the new knowledge and how it impacts them.

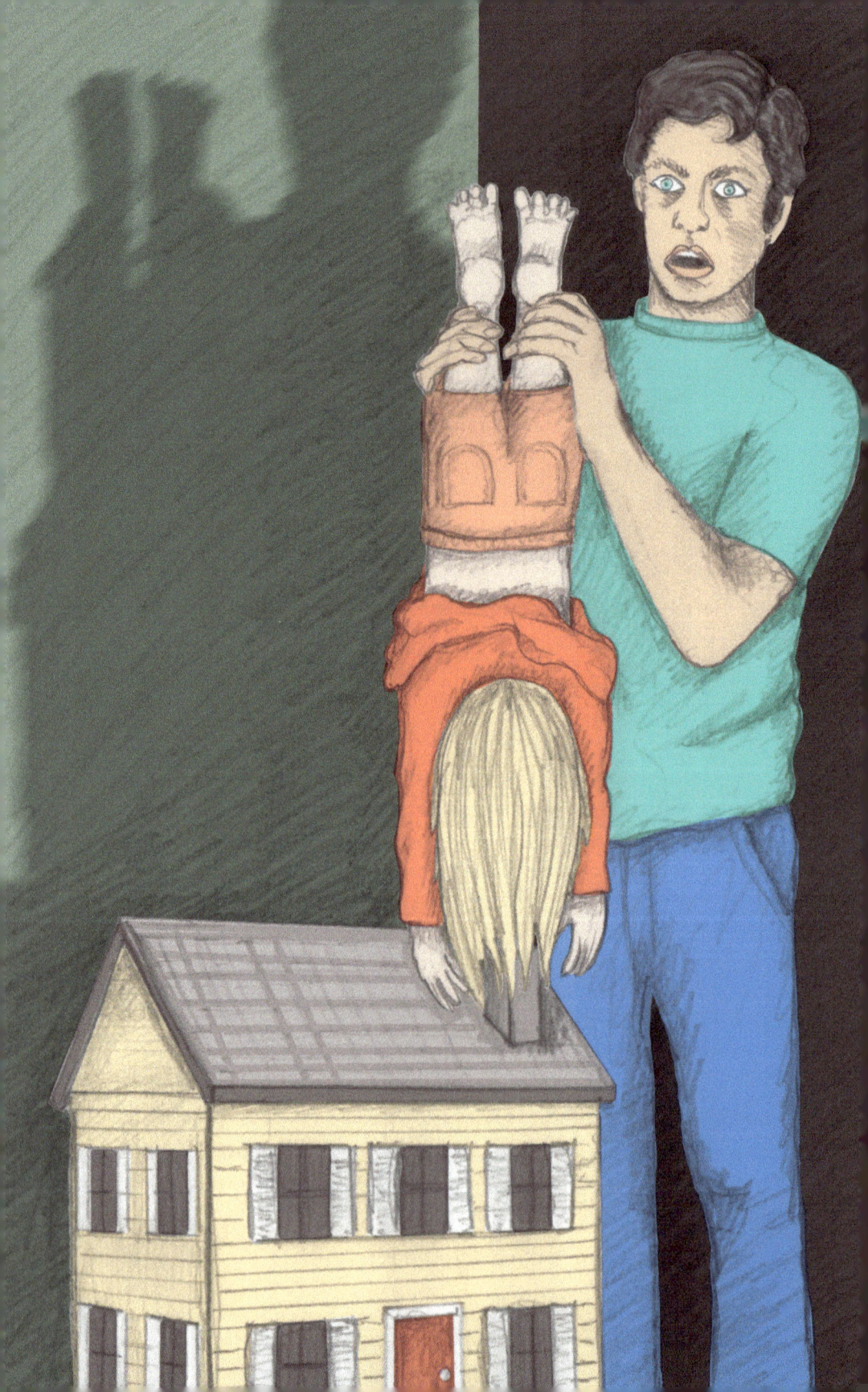

Invisible Trauma

Cheryl sought therapy because she was having difficulty in her relationships. She had trouble getting close, and trust was a huge issue for her. Physical intimacy was not difficult for her but, she struggled with emotional intimacy as a relationship deepened. She often sabotaged her relationships when they were going well. She was aware that she tended to choose unpredictable men, yet she didn't know why.

In exploring her childhood, she recalled a frightening incident at the age of six she had with her father. She loved her father, and she enjoyed her time with him. However, he had a temper and often got angry with her mom, but never with her.

One day, she was playing in her bedroom with her dollhouse. She was quiet, happy, and absorbed in her play. Suddenly, her father ran into her room yelling, picked her up by the feet, and dangled her over the dollhouse. It completely blindsided her. She thought she was going to die. The terrifying part for her was her father's glazed-over eyes. She could see that the loving father she knew was not inside this man holding her upside-down and shaking her.

I worked with her to revisit this trauma and access and express the terror she experienced.

She realized that by being blindsided, she had lost her trust in all aspects of life, not just with men. She had been playing happily in her bedroom. Safety was a non-issue because she was at home, so safety was a given. When this event happened, her world was deeply shaken. She didn't see it coming. She never felt safe again—anywhere. As a result, she started to be constantly on guard in preparation for something bad to happen. Life was serious business, and she didn't laugh very often.

We targeted the traumatic event, focusing on her fear of being blindsided by revisiting the memory and processing the sensations of terror and shock at that moment. We went through how the experience, like an earthquake, shook her belief system about life to the core. She came to know that she had developed the following mistaken belief: "I am never safe." We targeted this mistaken belief and tweaked it to: "Most of the time, I am safe, and if things turn upside-down, I will handle it."

As we did this, she healed from all aspects of the trauma. She started to trust in a way she never could before. She found she could be fully relaxed in different situations and around different people. She began to experience herself getting emotionally older.

When a relationship with a man was going well, she recognized that she was uncomfortable because she was on guard, anticipating pending chaos. She learned to breathe through these times, which helped her develop more neural pathways of well-being and a positive connection with her partner. As she went through this work, she started being attracted to different men—those who were predictable and solid. She also found that she attracted more predictable and solid men to her.

Dealing with Trauma

Going through the physical and emotional experiences of enduring a trauma is difficult. However, when one heals from a trauma, one can be stronger and wiser from going through it. Many people heal physically from a trauma but not emotionally. It is one thing to rebuild your home when it burns down, but it is another to feel safe again in your next home. To completely heal from a trauma, one needs to heal physically and emotionally.

Unhealed Trauma

Unhealed trauma can result in both cumulative and event trauma. Unhealed trauma interrupts and blocks *processing*. People get emotionally developmentally arrested at a young age—the age of the event.

Example of unhealed cumulative trauma:

Yayoi Kusama, a famous artist, drew from an early age. Her mother would sneak up behind her while she was engrossed in her art, grab her drawing, and rip it up. This trauma influenced how Kusama performed her art. She always worked very quickly as if she was going to be stopped at any minute.

Example of unhealed event trauma:

Kusama's parents owned a flower farm. When she was eight years old, she walked into a field of flowers as tall as her. She became a dot of colours among many other dots of colour. She lost her sense of self, lost her boundary, and ceased to exist as a human being. She was blindsided by this event trauma and became insecure about her existence. Her sense of existing became tenuous. She was afraid she might disappear at any time. This experience of ceasing-to-exist influenced her art as well. Much of her art consists of dots of colour. Her art spreads off the canvas, out of the room, and into nature. It has no boundary.

Trauma, per se, is not a problem. Instead, it is about how the person handles the trauma and what they do with it. Despite the trauma Kusama endured, she became a successful artist with an innovative approach to art that had never been done before.

Lack of Awareness

If you do not know you have unhealed trauma, you cannot treat it. You cannot deal with what you do not know. So many of us are little children, at various ages, dressed up in adult bodies. If the trauma is unhealed, the person may unconsciously repeat the trauma in different ways.

Example of repeating the same dynamics of the original trauma:

The Ghost of Trauma Past

Geoffrey, a man in his mid-60s, came to see me on his doctor's recommendation. Geoffrey had just retired. He and his third wife had been making plans for years to move to another part of the world and start a new life. His wife had been getting a degree, and she had just recently completed it. They were in the final stages of moving when she announced that she was leaving him. He was shocked and traumatized, which is why his doctor referred him to me.

In collecting his history, he told me about an incident he had always remembered from childhood. "When I was 7 years old, my mom and I lived with my grandparents while my dad was away at war. We got the news that my dad was coming home for good. He was going to buy a new car and get us. We could hardly wait for him to come.

He came with the new car, and after a few days, it was time to pack up and get ready to go. We packed up the car the night before we were set to leave. I woke up early the next morning, feeling excited. When I got downstairs, I found my mother crying. My parents had fought and broken up during the night. My dad had left without saying goodbye."

He told me this memory in a very matter-of-fact manner. He didn't cry or get distressed. He just reported it.

I told him that the event with his wife seemed the same as the event he had just recollected. He looked at me for a few moments. I could see the wheels going around in his head. Then he said to me, "Now, I know what happened in my other two marriages."

Geoffrey had recreated the unhealed trauma at age seven in all three of his marriages without knowing it. As a therapist, I can't specifically say how he did it, and it is not important to know; I just know that this happens with unhealed trauma. Putting together this information was a startling realization for him. Although he had remembered this childhood trauma, he had not healed from it. Therefore, we focused on healing the original trauma.

Example of a mistaken belief developed due to trauma:

Help! I Can't Stop What I'm Doing!

Nathalie, a woman in her mid-30s, came to see me. She was in distress. She had been married for 12 years, and for 10 of those years, she had been having an affair with another man. She said she didn't know why she was having an affair, and she desperately wanted to stop. She said she wanted children but couldn't have them until she decided which man she would be with.

We began therapy, and soon, she recalled a memory from the age of three. She had never recalled this memory before. She was at her brother's funeral, whom her father had accidentally run over with the car. She remembered standing between two big people looking across the gravesite. She saw the pain etched on her father's face. Unbeknownst to her, she was traumatized by her father's grief. Somehow, she decided to never have children so that she wouldn't have to experience the pain of ever losing them. I don't know how a child does this, it's certainly not in words/thoughts—but sensations.

Without Nathalie knowing it, the traumatic memory was stored in her Sensory Brain but was not available to her Logical Brain. The trauma was operating out of awareness. She had been managing her emotions in a unique way by having an affair, which prevented her from trying to get pregnant. The information was shared with the Logical Brain during therapy and could come into awareness. We targeted the trauma she experienced at the age of three and helped her access and express the fear and pain she felt at that time. As she breathed through the emotional pain, she processed the psychic pain she experienced at age three. Once she processed the trauma, the fear of pain and loss dissipated. She could live her life the way she wanted. Once she had healed from the trauma, she took action. She left her husband for the other man. However, that relationship didn't work out. She reconciled with her husband, and the last time I saw her, she was eight months pregnant with a big smile on her face.

Personal Story—Triggering Childhood Terror

I blacked out during my Clinical Oral exam.

On the day of my clinical oral exam, I arrived at the Counselling Psychology department well in time to set up the room for my presentation. It was scheduled to begin at 10:00 am.

As I was preparing, the professor from the department, who was NOT on my committee, came into the room. He asked me,"Did you know the time has been changed to 1:30 this afternoon."

Surprised, I said, "No I didn't." He turned and left. I was already very nervous and all I could think about was how am I going to keep myself calm until 1:30.

At 1:30 my exam began. I realized right away there was a problem, the professor, NOT on my committee, was angry with the other two but no one was talking about it or mentioning it. Even though I knew he was not angry with me—the charged atmosphere pushed me over my already highly nervous state. I dissociated.

I grew up with a troubled mother who would blow up and strap us kids. It was terrifying. I would dissociate during the strappings and gradually come back to awareness when it was over and she was calm again.

The tension between the professors was palpable and unspoken. I do not remember what happened.

At some point the professor who was the head of my committee said to me, "I'm concerned about what you're saying. At that moment, "I came back" I had totally blacked out, I had no idea of what I'd said. I worked to try to recover. I do not think they knew I was 'gone' because I kept talking and functioning. They passed me on my clinical work but failed my written paper. It was a horrible experience for me. I went home, crawled into bed and said, "That's it, I'm dropping out of the program." I pulled the covers over my head and went to sleep.

Needless to say, I didn't drop out but it was difficult to recover from the experience.

Dissociation

The extreme of disconnection from oneself is termed disso-ciation. The healthy function of dissociation is to help a person survive unbearable circumstances, such as war, a painful accident, a horrifying/near-death experience, etc. In family life or other situations with others, if a child or person cannot get away from difficult circumstances, dissociation helps them endure the intol-erable event. If people cannot get their bodies away from danger, they learn to dissociate and not feel the overwhelming physical and emotional sensations.

The first time, dissociation just happens, probably from the shock of what is going on, and afterward, the person tends to dissociate to endure difficult circumstances. They develop neural pathways for splitting off, disconnecting from their body sensations and emotional state.

Dissociation is more common than we realize. The mind splits off from reality to survive and cope, developing a robotic self that can operate in the world.

Dissociating can be like an on/off switch. A person can be living life normally until something happens and they are "gone." They have been triggered by something that reminds them of a dangerous event/situation. When it is safe, they return, remem-bering nothing of what happened or what was said and done.

Dissociation can also be on a continuum, like a light on a dimmer switch that gets gradually brighter or darker. To be slightly dissociated is to be present but feel fuzzy in one's thinking and/or numbness in one's body. This can get increasingly stronger until one is no longer present.

Trauma and the Brain

The corpus callosum is slow to develop in children. It is not fully developed until age seven. Due to its immaturity, information in one hemisphere may not get shared with the other. That information may be positive, negative, or neutral. That is, experiences that happen in childhood are often not shared with the Logical Brain, which means they cannot be *processed* and brought into awareness; this is often referred to as body memories. Even though the information is not in awareness, it can still influence behaviour in the present.

What frequently happens when we are struggling with a situation is that we have knowledge of the situation (Logical Brain), and we have a sense of the situation (Sensory Brain). We tend to spend more time thinking about it than sensing it. Thinking too much about the same situation is called ruminating; it is not productive. The information we need to *process* is in the Sensory Brain, limbic system, and body. We get the information by interrupting the ruminating and shifting into sensing (images, sensations, memories, etc.). As we stay with the sensations (Sensory Brain), the sensory information can then synthesize with the data from the Logical Brain, thus creating new perceptions.

Ruminating

Insights precipitate when both the Logical Brain and the Sensory Brain *process* the data. When *processing* is finished, the answers/solutions seem obvious. Often, we think, "Of course, why did I not realize that before/think of that before?"

Ruminating is a bad habit, but habits can be changed when you know what to do differently. To stop ruminating, you interrupt your thinking and shift to sensing—images, sounds, taste, touch, memories, etc.

When we experience sensations, we tend to leave the Sensory Brain and start *analyzing* the sensations and why we have them. It is okay to analyze; sometimes you will get the answer and stop ruminating. However, most of the time, the information in the Sensory Brain is required to get the answer.

To get the answers to your questions (Logical Brain), turn the question into one or more statements. For example, "Why am I lonely?" should be: "I am lonely." When I facilitate this exercise with clients, I ask them to resonate the statement within their bodies and see what sensations they experience. Then, I ask them to set that statement aside and make another statement. For example, "I am not lonely." I then ask my clients to resonate that statement with their bodies. From this exercise, my clients will get sensations from each statement—one statement will ring true, while the other will not. The statement that rings true gives them the answer to their question. In this way, the body and Sensory Brain answer the Logical Brain's question.

The Sensory Brain (plus the limbic system and body) create the emotions we experience, giving us sensations that guide us. We need this information to make intelligent, productive, healthy decisions. When you get into the habit of interrupting your thinking and shifting to your body, the new information precipitates quickly. When this becomes a new habit, you will stop ruminating.

Personal Story—I Can't Believe I Lived This Way for So Long

After 25 years, plus four years of courtship, my marriage ended in divorce. One day, I drove to a restaurant to meet my former husband to settle some financial issues. We had already been separated for a few months. As I got closer to the restaurant, my shoulders, upper arms, and neck got tenser and tenser. I became aware of it and had a sudden realization that I had lived many years in a chronic state of tension in my marriage. I felt relief that I no longer lived in that uncomfortable state.

Muscle Tension Spaghetti Analogy

Fully Relaxed Muscles

Semi-Contracted Muscles

Fully Contracted Muscles

The Physiology of Muscles

When we are tense, our muscles semi-contract. Muscles are made up of filaments that slide over each other. They bunch up into a ball when fully contracted, and they lengthen out and spread apart when relaxed. Muscles that are semi-contracted over time become painful creating chronic tension in our bodies. It takes a lot of energy to keep them semi-contracted. It is exhausting over time.

Personal Story—Now I Know What to Do!

One night, I was watching TV. I don't remember what I was watching, but I know it was not the news. I was relaxed. I had had a good day writing and a fun bike ride with my son, daughter-in-law, and grandson.

Suddenly, sensations came to my upper chest area, seemingly out of the blue. I immediately thought, "What on earth is this about?" I recognized these sensations because I had had them when I was stressed about something before.

I knew what to do.

I shifted out of thinking and questioning and focused on the sensations. I took deep breaths and breathed into them. The sensations quickly dissipated. I forgot about them.

Then, they came back stronger. This time, I sat up in my chair and leaned forward and breathed through them again, this time for longer. The sensations dissipated, and I forgot about them. They didn't return.

The next morning, I felt fine. They didn't return. I still don't know what they were about, but I assume that I was stressed about the deadline for writing this book. But it doesn't matter. I could handle the stress in a matter of minutes—no thinking, no ruminating, no scaring myself, no building of tension.

How to Heal from Trauma

When you are struggling with some issues, emotions, circumstances:

- Shift from thinking to sensing.

- Stay with the sensations and breathe through the waves.

- Do this as often as possible until the difficult time has passed.

There is no trauma to heal from.

How to Heal from Past Trauma

As mentioned before, people get emotionally developmentally arrested at the age they experience a traumatic event. To heal from past trauma, do not relive abusive memories. Instead, before the abuse happens, imagine receiving help or being rescued.

Some memories are a single snapshot of the traumatic event (Snapshot Memory), while others are a sequence of snapshots leading up to the traumatic event (Video Memory).

Mom was making us a special treat.
Why were we all crying?

Exercise for healing from a Snapshot Memory:

- Find a quiet place and time to revisit the memory. It takes time to do this.

- Visualize the memory and go back in time and relive the event.

- Be curious about everything in the "snapshot." Look at everything as though you have never seen it before. If you find yourself thinking/analyzing, notice it and return to visualizing and sensing.

- Notice your body sensations as you do this. Breathe into them.

- Every time you do it, you will probably recall more details.

- Spend some time doing this and then stop and do something else. Go outside in nature, play a musical instrument, exercise, bake, etc.

- Let it percolate.

Exercise for healing from a Video Memory:

Videos consist of a series of snapshots.

- Allow your mind to go through the sequence of snapshots.

- Allow the most troublesome moment in the sequence to come to the foreground.

- Let all the other moments fade into the background. Focus on this moment.

- Stay with any sensations you experience and "let them be."

- What is, is. You are having these sensations. Breathe into them.

- Relive that moment as best you can.

- This is how you access your younger self.

- Let that moment fade into the background and let the next more troublesome moment float to the foreground.

- Repeat.

- Let that moment fade into the background and let the next more troublesome moment float to the foreground.

- Repeat until there are no more left.

- Spend some time doing this and then stop and do something else. Go outside in nature, play a musical instrument, exercise, bake, etc.

- Let it percolate.

Often, other memories come to you while you are doing this. Do the same with each memory. These memories are linked together even though they may not seem to be. There will be a pattern to them. This is positive. It relates to your modus operandi.

When you access your younger self with your current age self, you bring together two important databases. Your younger self did not have an adult self, so it could not know or realize many things. However, your current age self brings all your knowledge and awareness to this experience. It is like looking at old information with new eyes. Your brain will integrate the information. Your adult self makes sense of your experience in a way your younger self never could.

Other ways to heal from past traumas:

Draw the memory:

- On a giant post-it note, draw your memory. Do this standing up to access the Sensory Brain where memory is stored. (Let go of the need to draw well. This is not about drawing. This is about accessing, expressing, and *processing* feelings).

Enact the memory:

- Create the memory-scape in the room you are in.

- Re-enact each part of the memory. Be each person, animal, furniture, natural force, etc.

Reclaiming the Power Within

A client (age 17) had a recurring nightmare wherein she was happily walking along the beach on a nice day. Suddenly, a tsunami hit the shore, washing her away, and there was nothing she could do about it.

In therapy, I asked her to imagine my office as the dreamscape. I asked her to be herself, walking along the beach. She did as I told her, and she experienced this happy, pleasant state she was in. Then, I asked her to be the tsunami wave. She pretended to be the humongous wave coming onto the shore where she was happily walking. In the middle of the action of being the wave, she suddenly had an "aha moment."

"This is my father! This is what my father does to me!"

This was new information to her. It took her a while to process the new awareness.

Therapy then shifted to helping her hold her own with her father. The tsunami represented her power, which she had disowned. Part of the therapy focused on helping her re-own her power, which was immense and frightening to her, yet exciting too.

Deconstruct the Old and Reconstruct the New

Jupe recalled the following memory:

"I am nine years old. My brother, who is seven years old, has just read my diary. I go to my mother to tell her what he did, but she does nothing about it! I remember my brother standing there with a smirk on his face."

In this memory, Jupe is passive, powerless, and frozen in time. Here, Jupe can be the editor of her life.

Scenario A: I tell my mother, and she sends my brother to his room for the rest of the day. I bake cookies with my mom.

Scenario B: I catch my brother about to read my diary and pull his pants down. He is embarrassed and runs away. I take my diary and find a better place to hide it.

Scenario C: My brother runs up behind me and lifts me up, and carries me outside on his shoulders. We go to the gelato place and get ice cream. He pays. We have fun together.

Scenario D: I'm just about to tell my mom that my brother has read my diary, and suddenly, Wonder Woman flies into the room and takes me out of the house. We're flying through the air. It is wonderful! I am free!

The revised memories contaminate the original memory, helping it to deconstruct. It is still there but no longer has the power it once had.

In the revised scenarios, Jupe is in charge of her life in different ways. Moving forward, she is empowered to create her own life.

Be the editor of your early life:

- Imagine a recurring nightmare turning out differently.

- Let go of logic.

- Re-enter the nightmare at any point and change the outcome to have a positive outcome with a positive feeling tone with pleasant sensations. It is no longer a nightmare but a positive dream.

- Create at least three different scenarios. More is even better.

How to Heal from Unknown Trauma

As I said previously, if you do not know that you are traumatized, there is nothing you can do to heal it. If you have unhealed trauma and do not know it, that means it is operating under-ground, i.e., in your subconscious.

Unhealed trauma, kind of like a virus, replicates itself over and over in different ways. It is not a problem if the trauma is healed because the psychic wound is healed; it can no longer replicate itself.

It is common for people to remember the trauma but still not realize it is unhealed. Or, if they realize it is unhealed trauma, they do not know how to heal it.

In circumstances of childhood trauma, people can evoke memories by:

- Looking at photos of themselves as children.

- Talking to parents, grandparents, and other relatives about their memories and absorbing the feedback about their perceptions of the same memories.

- Talking to members in the community they grew up in, including teachers, neighbours, former classmates, etc.

- Looking at their old yearbooks, scrapbooks, newspaper articles, etc.

- Visiting their childhood home(s), schools, and communities.

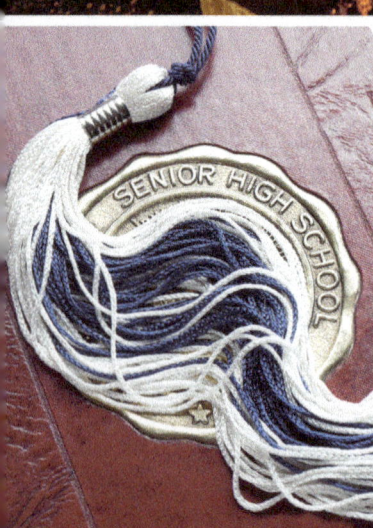

While exploring your childhood, you may or may not come across any trauma. Most people have trauma while growing up, some of which is healed and some not. It is important not to minimize or dismiss unhealed traumas because they seem small and inconsequential compared to others.

Another benefit of exploring your childhood is that you may find events that gave you joy, events from which you learned valuable lessons, or events that remind you of the good times you had. Positive memories can remind you of internal resources you have and can draw on going forward. That is, you already have neural pathways for positive experiences that are dormant; they can be brought to the foreground and be nurtured.

When clients have *processed* old traumas, I have found that they start remembering positive memories they never or rarely remembered before. It is as if they were buried under the crud of unhealed trauma.

Healed Trauma

- Remember traumatic incident.

- Remember that the feelings/sensations were painful but do not feel the pain in the present.

- Forget traumatic incident completely.

- Do not repeat trauma.

Unhealed Trauma

- Remember traumatic incident.

- Re-experience the painful feelings/sensations when remembered and recall them in the present.

- Repress traumatic incident.

- Keep repeating trauma.

Exercise

How to work with a memory that records a past trauma:

- Find a quiet place and a time you will not be disturbed.

- Settle into a comfortable position.

- Start by focusing on your breathing (let go of thinking).

- Allow the memory of the trauma to float to the foreground.

- Let the part of the memory that is most bothersome float to the foreground.

- What do you notice in terms of sensations?

- Where in your body do you experience the sensations?

- As best as you can, articulate what the sensations are like: pleasant/unpleasant; tense/relaxed; /hollow/full; tired/energized; calm/agitated; hard/soft; narrow/wide, etc.

- Stay with the sensations and breathe into them. Imagine sending the sensations oxygen or something else that is positive.

- Breathe through the waves of sensations until they are gone.

How to Help Others Help Themselves

When people articulate their history, they often relive their memories or parts of their memories in the telling. They often get insights. They frequently remember more details of the memory and/or remember a different memory linked to the first one. They may even realize the memory is not accurate.

Personal Story—I Realize That I Did It to Protect Myself

One time, in therapy, I recalled this memory:

When I was three years old, we lived in a house with no electricity and no running water. It was winter and very cold. I was in the bath, and I had to pee. My mom made me get out of the tub and go outside to the outhouse. As I recalled the memory aloud to my therapist, I visualized the details in the wooden boards with knots and cracks that lined the path to the outhouse.

I suddenly became quiet, and my therapist asked, "What is happening?"

I explained to her that I suddenly realized that my mother would never make a three-year-old go outside in the winter. My mom was tough but would never do that. It was at this moment that I realized my memory was not true. Instead, I had put together information from a different age since I had walked those planks to the outhouse many times as an older child. I had created a false memory to tell myself that my mom could be mean.

Often, people feel validated when someone listens to their story, as though they matter in some way, even though nothing changes. Listening to someone's story with interest validates the person somehow, even if the memory was false.

Memories are not about truth or fact; they are about perception and meaning.

- Talk to people about their childhood in-depth:

- Be curious: "Tell me more about that."

- Show interest: "Help me understand how that came about, what you learned, etc."

- Show positive reinforcement. "Wow! That was tough on you. You were just a kid!"

- Show compassion: "I'm sorry that happened to you."

- Let go of the facts and listen to their story. Listen with your heart!

- Share how you feel as they tell their story: "I have goosebumps listening to that. I am shocked that someone would even do/say that."

- Let the story unfold as the teller tells it. Do not make it about you. If you want/need to share your story, tell it later (see story on page 120).

- AVOID: Analyzing, giving advice, playing Devil's Advocate, judging negatively, questioning the truth/fiction of what they are saying.

Key Takeaways:

- **Unhealed trauma is recreated in the present; healed trauma is not.**

- **As people heal from trauma, their emotional age catches up with their current age.**

- **Overcoming trauma makes us wiser.**

- **Blindsiding is a severe form of trauma that is seldom recognized.**

CHAPTER NINE

Realign Your Energy, Reclaim Your Life

*"Eventually, order goes into chaos
and out of chaos a new order emerges."* —Bea Mackay

There are many things in this life that we can do nothing about. Many things are too overwhelming to change. However, the one thing we can change is our relationship with ourselves. There are two parts of self—the body, which I refer to as the Experiencing Self, and the thinking part, which I refer to as the Critic. A Critic can be constructive/productive or destructive/unproductive.

Experiencing Self

We are living, breathing organisms. We came into existence, arriving on this planet through no choice of our own. Our organism has wants and needs; it has likes/dislikes, talents, strengths/weaknesses, interests/disinterests, and sensitivities. Our bodies create sensations that inform us we are alive and influence our thoughts and actions. It experiences the sensations of emotions. Once living entities come into existence, they are programmed to survive and procreate.

Critic

We have a thinking part of our brain that thinks about our organism. We can think about the past, present, and future of our existence. Other creatures and entities cannot think about themselves. They mostly live in the moment. The Critic has standards and values. It analyzes emotions, but it does not sense them.

Each one of us has a relationship with ourselves. It is as though we are all identical twins—one part of us thinks (Critiquer), and the other part senses (Experiencing Self). We relate to ourselves. When we relate well to ourselves, our energy is aligned. Aligned, the two parts of ourselves—the Experiencing Self and the Critic—work together as a team; they give and receive love, support, comfort, compassion, kindness, cheerleading, forgiveness, and more. The standards and values of the Critic are aligned with the Experiencing Self's wants and needs. In this way, a person's energy is all available to live life.

When we relate poorly with ourselves, our energy splits and is pitted against itself. When this happens, the split-off energy is not

available for us to use. We get tired easily from the inner struggle. Gradually, more and more energy is split off until there is not enough energy to live life. I am always amazed at what people can accomplish and make happen when most of their energy is invested in the internal battle.

When the relationship with the self is negative and harmful, the Critic treats the Experiencing Self badly. It berates, puts down, humiliates, shames, sabotages, undermines, embarrasses, stonewalls, and exhausts the Experiencing Self. To survive, the Experiencing Self must brace against the Critic; thereby, wasting more energy.

When our energy is aligned, we *process* our emotions as we need to and when it is appropriate. As emotions come into awareness, we acknowledge them and breathe through the sensations. If it is not a convenient or appropriate time to do so, we will *manage* the sensations until we can *process* them.

When our energy is opposed, we minimize and deny what feelings, meanings, and sensations we are experiencing, thereby treating ourselves badly. Self-esteem is a by-product of how we treat ourselves. When we treat ourselves well, our self-esteem rises. When we treat ourselves badly, our self-esteem plummets. What we can control is how we interact with ourselves.

There are different styles for interacting with ourselves.

The Difference Between Treating Ourselves *Well* and Treating Ourselves *Badly*

Styles of treating ourselves *well* include:

Healthy selfishness
(caring for yourself as you care for others too)

Cajoling (being able to laugh at oneself in a caring way)

Encouraging/inspiring/validating
(being your own best cheerleader/coach)

Supportive (enjoys and is proud of achievements)

Understanding/compassionate

Self-aware/observant (connected with self)

Flexibility with oneself
(can be firm or soft depending on the situation)

Spiritual (GOD IS LOVE, I am inherently good,
I make mistakes, and I can ask for forgiveness and get it)

Bravery (healthy advocacy)

Styles of treating ourselves *badly* include:

Unhealthy selfishness
(only caring about yourself, not others)

Taking yourself too seriously in a self-disparaging way

Undermining/doubting/sabotaging/invalidating/shaming/
blaming/criticizing/scaring/terrifying/threatening

Unsupportive/condemning/contemptuous/callous
(discounts and dismisses their own achievements)

Lacks self-understanding and/or compassion for oneself

Unaware/blind (disconnected from self)

Rigid with oneself
(cannot adjust to different situations)

Religious (FEAR THE LORD, I am a sinner, I am evil, I will be
punished, I am fatally flawed, and I can never forgive myself)

Cowardly (cannot advocate for oneself)

I'm All Right!

Lillian, a widow in her mid-50s, came for help because she was afraid for her health. If she felt dizzy, she was sure she had a brain tumour. If she was thirsty or went to the bathroom too often, she was convinced she had diabetes. If she felt upset in her stomach or tightness in her throat, she believed she had cancer. She was literally scaring herself to death.

She knew what she was doing, but she talked about it as though she were a victim and powerless to do anything different. She had tried to stop but couldn't help herself. This was all going on inside her head. I wanted her to experience what she was doing to herself, so instead of talking to me about what she does inside her head, I had her talk to herself. I told her to have the two parts of her interact, and I facilitated the interaction.

The attacking part (Critic) told her she would get sick and how she would get sick. The other part (Experiencing Self) defended her and explained herself. The Critic didn't listen.

Instead, the Critic brushed aside what the Experiencing Self said and intensified the attack. The Critic got bigger and stronger, and the Experiencing Self got smaller and weaker. Finally, the Experiencing Self gave up in despair. The Critic looked at me and said in a strong, clear tone, "See, I told you, this is what I do." It was clear that she had a lot of power but that the power was destructive.

I told her she was "at war" with herself and had a bad habit of attacking herself without realizing it. Habits can be changed; even bad habits can be changed.

First, she needed to increase her awareness. I gave her an exercise to do at home. She was to "catch herself" doing the scaring.

The next week, she came back and said in astonishment, "I do that to myself hundreds of times a day. I had no idea how bad it was!" Her awareness increased, and she began to take ownership and responsibility for her unhealthy treatment.

This time, we worked to interrupt the attacking and establish new behaviours instead. Her homework was to catch when she was scaring herself and implement the new behaviours.

We discovered in this process that she didn't have a life. Of course, if you are convinced that you'll die every day, you don't make plans to work, travel, or socialize.

I learned she was a widow. Her second husband, whom she deeply loved, had died several years ago, and she had been grieving his death ever since. She was not interested in a new relationship. She had only a few friends, and she was retired.

Our next focus became finding a new life for her with people and activities she enjoyed.

After several months, she found a church, which she found welcoming, and joined in their activities. She would stay after the service to mingle with the members and get to know them. She rediscovered an old interest—singing—and joined the choir.

I continued to coach her on how to change her "bad habit" of scaring herself. Her Critic was often interrupted, which helped the Experiencing Self get stronger and emotionally healthier. The energy between the two, which had been opposed, slowly started to realign. The inner war died down, although not completely.

She had more energy to focus on building her new life and reconnecting with old friends.

A few months later, she came to therapy with news. She calmly told me, "I am fine." Surprised and intrigued, I said, "Tell me about it."

After our last session together, she said that she stopped at an intersection on her walk home. As she waited for the light to turn green, a car came along, which she described as a muscle car, and she noticed something dangling from the rearview mirror. The song blaring from the car was "I'm All Right" by Kenny Loggins. Suddenly, she just knew she was fine. "There was a 'click' in my head," she said. "Now, if I start to worry too much about my health, I just remember the object dangling from the mirror, and I know I am all right." The 'click' in Lillian's head was the new formation of neural pathways which gave her pleasant calming sensations to which she gave new meaning.

Lillian's brain had reorganized itself. We had explored her relationship with herself. We found out exactly how she was scaring herself and helped her become more aware of her inner dialogue. We started interrupting and changing her "bad habit," that is, her pattern of scaring herself and then introduced new behaviours for her to do. Putting new behaviours in place helps people let go of old behaviours.

Mistaken Beliefs

Mistaken beliefs are firm beliefs that are not true but are embedded in our way of being (modus operandi). We can know logically and rationally that we matter (Logical Brain), but our experiences (Sensory Brain) in childhood are that we did not matter, and we believe our experiences.

Accurate Beliefs	Mistaken Beliefs
I matter	I do not matter
I am enough	I am never enough
I am special/important	I am worthless
I am not alone	I am on my own
I am good (in God's eyes)	I am evil
Others are mostly good	Others are bad
I am OK just the way I am	I am not OK. There is something wrong with me.

Identity

People tend to develop an identity very early in life. According to birth order theory, the first two children tend to polarize. If the eldest is the easy child, the second child is the difficult child or vice versa. When the eldest child is born, they have their parents all to themselves. They do not have to compete with anyone for parental resources. When the second child is born, they are born competing from the moment they arrive in the family. Once the second child enters the family, the first child needs to start competing for parental resources.

Many factors influence this pattern, including the age between siblings, the energy level of each child, passiveness/activeness of each child, circumstances at the time of birth, the health of each child, etc. If more children come along, there are more resources in the family, so later-born children tend not to polarize. Older children tend to be more responsible, probably because they need to look after and help younger siblings, and the youngest tend to be more irresponsible. The youngest tend to be irresponsible because they are used to others doing things for them and often are "babied" by their parents. When they procrastinate, someone else is more likely to do chores and take responsibility. Sometimes, the youngest children supersede their older siblings. This can be very difficult for older siblings depending on how each family members feels about themselves.

In families, children often develop an identity—the "good" child, the "difficult" child, the "clumsy" child, the "helpless" child, the "genius" child, the "musician," the "athlete," the "introvert," the "chatterbox," the "witty" one, the "go-to person," the "clown," the "misfit," the "idiot," etc. Often, these identities play out in the larger world, starting at school and then at work. Sometimes they last a lifetime. Based on personality and circumstances, they often change in adulthood.

If a family value exists within a family, such as athleticism, intelligence, responsibility, helping others, artistic or musical talents, all children would often take on the family value, but usually in different ways.

Dr. Galen, the doctor who wrote the first medical text, had twelve children. They all became doctors with different specialties. When they got together at family gatherings, and one of the children got injured, they had too many diagnoses.

Often, there is a rebel in the family. In a family of responsible citizens, there may be one delinquent. In dealing with the delinquent, the parental resources get used up, and the good children get ignored and neglected. Children of doctors are often ignored because they are healthy. Or, some families are on the wrong side of the law but have one child who is a good citizen. I call this kind of rebel the "white sheep of the family."

Celine Dion is the youngest of fourteen children. She was put on the dining room table as a tiny tot and sang to her siblings. She was her mother's baby; that is, there were no more babies to take her place. From the age of two, she was singing to a huge crowd— her siblings. She superseded her siblings. Her identity formed at an early age. She was a performer/singer.

From the beginning of history, the eldest children have taken on parental standards and values and inherited the bulk of the parental assets. Later-born children have become rebels, explorers, creators, artists, degenerates, and wastrels.

People are creative. They develop unique styles of how they treat themselves. They can treat themselves well (i.e., being kind to themselves, supportive of themselves, forgiving of themselves, etc.). In this way, their energy is aligned and available to live life. Or, they can treat themselves badly (i.e., disparage themselves, shame themselves, invalidate themselves, etc.). In this way, their energy is opposed and is not available to live life.

That's Outside My Comfort Zone

Caroline came for therapy because she was unhappy in her marriage. It was her second marriage, and she had been in it for 15 years. She felt stuck. She would swing back and forth from wanting to leave to wanting to stay. Whenever she wanted to leave and got to the place where action was required, she would swing back to wanting to stay, saying, "It's not so bad." Yet, staying also required action in the form of commitments of time and money, making plans for holidays, etc. She didn't want to take these actions, so she would swing back to wanting to leave.

Since the swings back and forth were initiated by the need to take action, we focused around her avoidance of taking action. I would make suggestions for her to experiment with. For example, I suggested she go to open houses to see what type of place she might like to move to. She said she couldn't do it because it was too uncomfortable for her. I said she didn't have to talk to a real estate person or talk to a bank about mortgages; she just had to start the process by going into and exploring units on the market. I suggested she take a friend who enjoys this type of activity with her. However, this was also outside her comfort zone as she had not told any of her friends about wanting to leave her marriage.

She was unable and unwilling to take any action to end the relationship. I told her that as long as she was still in the relationship, she could explore actions that would improve the relationship. For example, couples counselling, carving out more time with her husband, taking more holidays alone, etc. Going for couples counselling and taking trips by herself were outside her comfort zone. We explored small actions she could take to improve her situation in the marriage. As long as they were small, she would do them, and ultimately, she found a way to be in the marriage that was not good but at least less bad for her. She had become a prisoner of her own comfort zone.

Below are three examples of how people have a negative relationship with themselves:

1. Comfort Zone

When people say that they are uncomfortable, they are saying they cannot tolerate the sensations they feel when trying something new, so they stay in their comfort zones. However, they do not realize that their comfort zone is getting smaller and smaller. Eventually, they become a prisoner of their own comfort zone.

Research has found that people can tolerate a 7% change from their current behaviours. Therefore, I always tell my clients to go 7% more beyond their comfort zones and breathe through the sensations. By doing so, they expand their comfort zones because by *processing* their emotions, they do not have uncomfortable sensations to *manage*.

2. Risk-taking

Risk-takers want to experience certain sensations (i.e., ecstatic, thrilling, exciting, new, different, etc.). They are driven to participate in activities where they will experience intense, thrilling, or terrifying sensations to achieve a sense of aliveness. When people are disconnected from themselves, they feel numb, so they seek activities to feel alive.

It Makes Me Feel So Alive!

Martin was a thrill-seeker in all aspects of his life. He sought out the sensations of excitement. His work was in start-up internet companies, and he had taken two companies from start-up to getting listed on the stock market, and now, he was on his third company. He had made millions, and money was not an issue for him. He thoroughly enjoyed the emotional roller-coaster ride his work took. He did rock climbing, scuba diving, and rode his motorcycle. His favourite movies were horror and action. He couldn't sit still.

He was not aware of how exhausted he was.

He said he was active because he felt numb and dead when he was not doing anything.

He had a difficult childhood with a harsh father in the military. He said he survived by putting his emotions in a box and stashing them in the back of his mind. The problem with this was that he didn't feel human. When he took risks, he felt alive. The sensations he experienced with risks let him know he was alive.

3. Victimization

Victimization is the *process* of making others powerless by overpowering them, disparaging them, being physically and emotionally abusive, violating boundaries, etc. When people are victimized as children, they are powerless to fight their oppressors, but they have energy, which has nowhere to go, so it is turned against the self, and they develop a lifestyle of victimizing themselves.

I MATTER
THE SECOND-MOST.

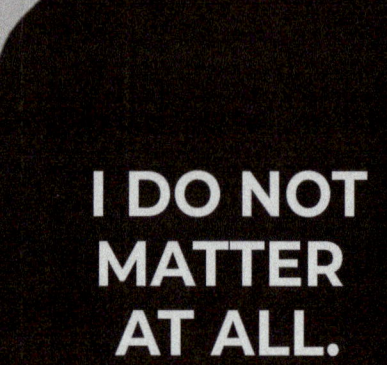
I DO NOT
MATTER
AT ALL.

I MATTER
THE MOST.

I MATTER.

I MATTER.

I MATTER
SOMEWHAT.

I MATTER, BUT
NOT SO MUCH.

I MATTER A LOT!

I Only Count If I Care For Others

Samantha came to therapy because she couldn't influence any of her family members in the way she wanted and needed. She wanted to be taken seriously as a family member who mattered too. She was tiny, short, and not attractive. She had little presence. Her strength was her intellect; she was brilliant but didn't know it.

Samantha was the middle child of three children. She had a brother who was two years older and a sister who was two years younger. When she was six, her mother left the family and married another man. He was rich.

Samantha's mother did not want her children to live with her and her new husband, so she left them with her mother and father. Samantha's grandparents were not wealthy, but they were ambitious. They had a house and rented out most of the rooms to strangers, hoarding the money, skimping on food, and buying more property. The five of them slept in one of the bedrooms in the home. Samantha found it crowded and uncomfortable. Her mother was well-off, but she never financially contributed to her children's care. She did not get involved in their upbringing or education. No one cared about Samantha or her well-being. She did extremely well in school, but her accomplishments were never acknowledged, encouraged, or celebrated.

Eventually, she achieved a B.A. and a law degree. But even these degrees did not convince her of her intelligence. She went on to earn a Master's degree in Law. She articled for a firm of lawyers whom she respected. They took advantage of her ability and paid her poorly. However, her lack of presence in the courtroom took the opposing lawyers off-guard as they underestimated her capability. Even the judges were surprised at her expertise. Samantha worked hard and won most of *her cases. Finally, Samantha realized and accepted that she was intelligent and competent as a lawyer. She could not dismiss or minimize their opinions about her because she respected them as lawyers.*

However, she still couldn't get love, care, or acknowledgment from her mother or any family members, the people she desperately wanted a connection with.

She was a victim in her family, work, and of others who took advantage of her. She was starved for love and attention, and the more she sought it out from her mother and other family members, the more she was victimized.

In therapy, we focused on helping her reclaim her power, setting clear boundaries with others and owning her abilities and expertise.

Eventually, she severed all ties with her family because they continued to be contemptuous of her. She did not stay at the law firm where she articled. She eventually started her own practice in a niche area.

She views herself as surviving victimization.

Anger

When people get angry, it helps them make what they want happen or prevents what they do not want to happen.

Underlying anger forms the sensations of vulnerability, which can range from slight to extreme. No one likes to feel the sensations of vulnerability, so most people avoid or deflect from them by talking about something else, focusing on a task, or worrying about their aches or pains.

Anger expressed negatively can devastate a child of any age, especially when young. Anger can destroy relationships and ruin things of value. People can hurt others when they get angry.

Anger has gotten a bad rap. There are times when it is appropriate and productive to get angry. It is healthy to express anger in ways that channel the energy out of the body—ways that do not hurt the self or anyone else and do not damage anything of value (e.g., chopping wood, ripping up a phone book, pounding in nails, scrubbing a floor—any sport that involves an attacking type motion, such as soccer, baseball, tennis, squash, lacrosse, etc.)

But often, getting angry can be dangerous, even embarrassing. Knowing the difference and having the impulse control to carry out the choice are helpful.

Most important of all is what a person says and how a person acts when they are angry.

No One Is Going to See Me Cry!

Florence came for therapy because of a problem at work. Her boss told her to get help managing her anger. She reluctantly came because she was afraid of losing her job.

Florence was full of resentment toward her boss and coworkers. I listened to her complaints and reflected back the vulnerability underlying them. She was hurt by everyone in her life and managed these feelings by getting angry. No one was going to see her cry! As I continued to reflect back the hurt she felt, she became less angry and more emotional. Then she burst into tears. She was able to cry for the first time in years.

She talked about her childhood and how her father was always angry. He never showed any emotion aside from anger, and she couldn't get close to him. Her mom was afraid of her dad and was always depressed, so Florence couldn't get close to her either. She had a very lonely childhood. She learned to manage her emotions like her dad. She was contemptuous of her mom and didn't want to be like her. She suppressed any emotion by getting angry. No one could get close to her either.

I worked with Florence to help her shift from managing her emotions to processing them. Eventually, she could come into her own and interact with others in a way she had never been able to do before. She stopped being an angry person. She started making friends and doing better at work.

How to Change Your Relationship with Yourself

As said previously, there is a lot you can do nothing about in this world. However, the one thing we can control is our relationship with ourselves. We are living, breathing creatures (Experiencing Self) trying to survive, cope, and thrive as best as we can. We have a thinking self (Critic) that can analyze and interact with our Experiencing Self.

Our early experiences in life shape us. Growing up, we adapt. We take on our parents' standards and values or reject them. We develop a way of being in the world as we get through childhood. This way of being consists of many habits—some positive and some negative. We can keep the habits we find constructive and productive, and we can let go of and change the habits that we find destructive and negative in some way. We can become all we can become; we can develop our unique personalities to their fullest.

Bea's Trees

Step 1: Identify the type of interaction: positive, productive, constructive, healthy, neutral, destructive, unproductive, and unhealthy.

We each develop our style and personality. Identify your style and the ways you treat yourself that you like and nurture those more. Then identify the ways you treat yourself that are not emotionally or physically healthy.

Your energy is like an invisible force. Just like a tree in the wind (force), the environment can cause habits that can be destructive, unproductive, or healthy. A healthy tree thrives in a nurturing environment (good treatment). While the wind is still an invisible force, a healthy tree is flexible and sways in the wind.

Step 2: Interrupt the Critic

When the Critic interacts with the Experiencing Self, the Experiencing Self has sensations in the body. When the Critic treats the Experiencing Self badly, the Experiencing Self experiences unpleasant sensations. These sensations are cues that let you know that the Critic needs to be interrupted.

When a wheel is rolling along on the ground but it is going in the wrong direction, you need to bring it to a stop first before changing the direction. We need to bring the negative Critic to a halt before we can get it to be positive. We do this by interrupting the Critic's prevailing force against the self and developing productive new behaviors to do instead. Without new behaviors the self defaults to the only program it has.

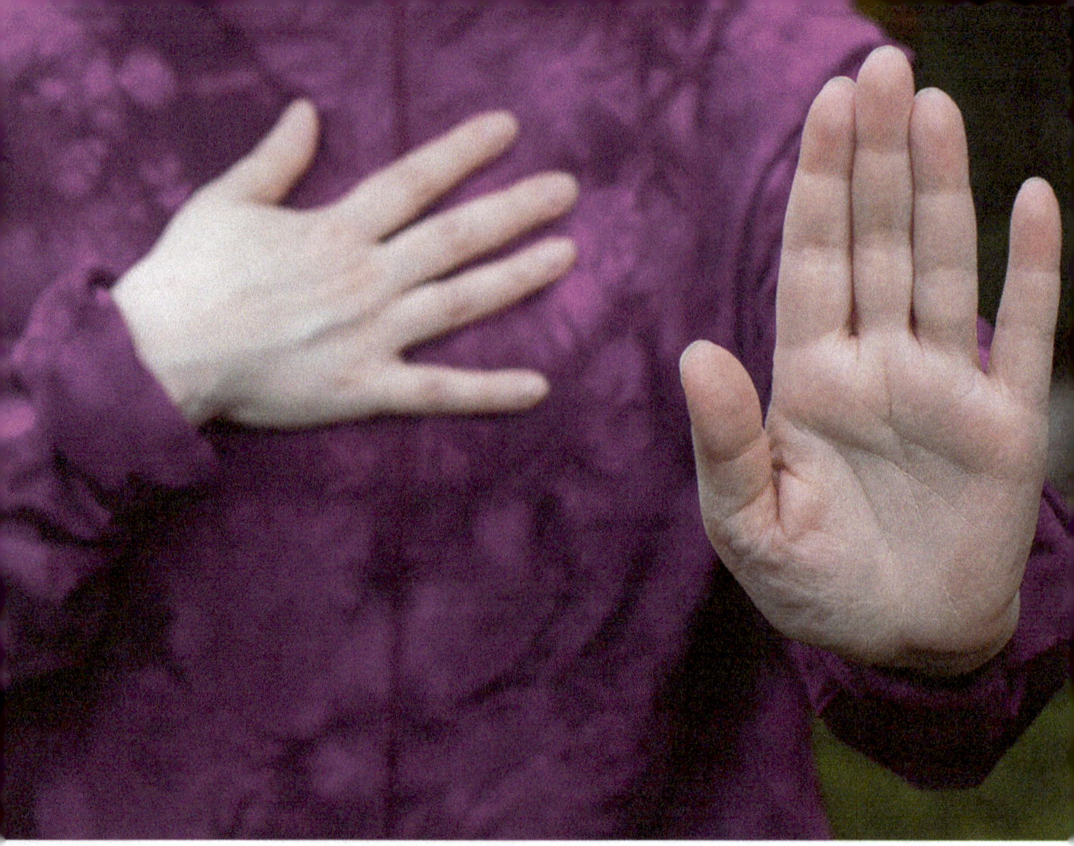

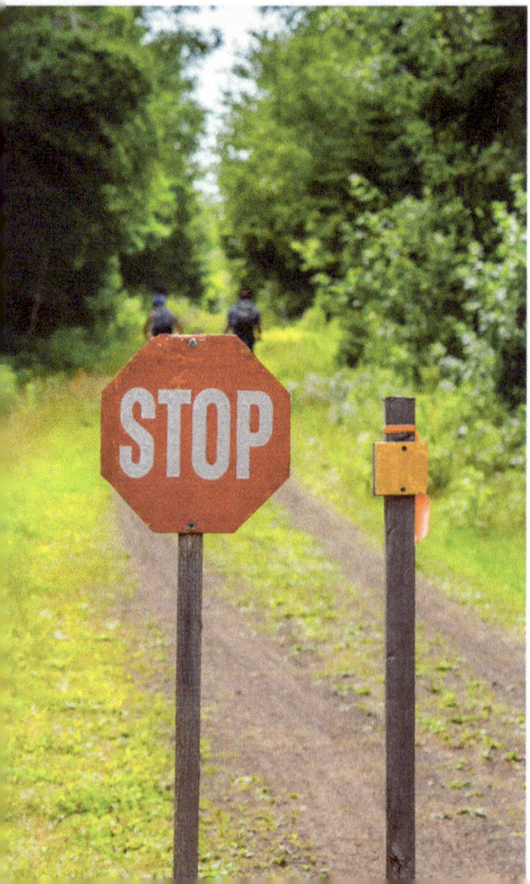
STOP

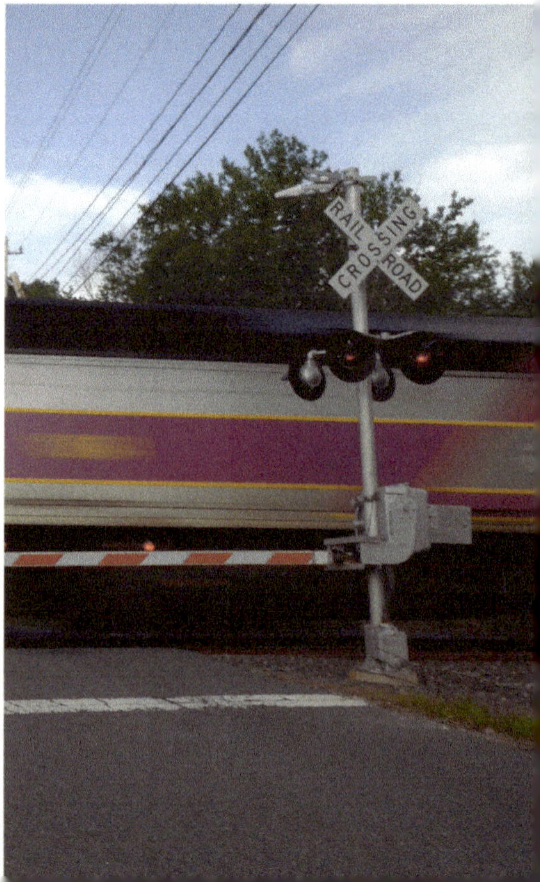
RAIL ROAD
CROSSING

Step 3: Put new behaviours in place

The Experiencing Self imagines something that means STOP to the Critic. For example, a hand gesture, a stop sign, etc. The Critic then receives the signal and puts itself into wait mode. For example, wait mode can be a memory of waiting at a railway crossing for a train to go by, waiting to get on the plane in the boarding lounge, lying in a hammock, etc.

Step 4: The path to change

The choice point is the point where you are aware that the old pattern is happening. At this point, you can decide between your old pattern or new behaviours. If you decide to repeat old patterns, do so deliberately because when you do something with awareness that you typically do automatically, your brain has to work differently. That is what we are trying to do—shake up the old pattern so that the new pattern can be established.

On the other hand, every time you choose to put new behaviours in place, you create new neural pathways. With more new neural pathways, it gets easier; however, as with everything else, you need to practice, practice, practice.

How to Let Go

You can tell yourself to stop beating yourself up, shaming yourself, lying to yourself, etc. (these are Logical Brain directions). However, it usually does not work unless you put new behaviours in place. You need to use the Sensory Brain cues to shift into the Sensory Brain with new behaviours.

Advocating for the Experiencing Self

The more emotionally healthy people are, the more readily their Critic will soften. People who have struggled in childhood with difficult relative(s), teacher(s), coaches, and other significant people often develop Critics that are just as difficult, sometimes even more difficult, than the real people.

When the Critic refuses to soften, and the Experiencing Self cannot find the strength even with a therapist's support to stand up to the Critic, the therapist needs to intervene and advocate for the Experiencing Self. The therapist needs to stop the client's abuse of the self. This creates the experience of being advocated for, which they missed out on growing up, and creates new neural pathways essential to protecting oneself and holding boundaries.

In this case, the person's own Critic is an introjection of an extremely abusive or emotionally disturbed parent(s), sibling, or another significant person. One parent may be extremely abusive and domineering, while the other may be emotionally disturbed. Or, the other parent may be absent somehow, perhaps through withdrawal, drunkenness, desertion, or overworking.

Exercises

1. How to balance Sensory Brain and Logical Brain functioning:

   - Catch yourself thinking.

   - Do a body scan for sensations.

   - Stay with that for 3-5 seconds and go back to thinking.

   - Repeat.

   - Try to stay longer with your sensations each time.

2. How to interrupt the habit of negative thinking by switching to behaviours:

   - Interrupt negative thinking (beating yourself up, feeling guilty, etc.).

   - Shift to an action (stomp your feet, chop up vegetables, rip up a magazine, shake a pillow, etc.).

3. When you sense something—a twinge in your side, a headache, fatigue, stiff neck, etc.—try to stay with the sensations and be curious how and where in your body you sense them before you go to the Logical Brain to figure out what the sensations might be. If you are disappointed, how do you know you are disappointed? Go to the sensations for verification.

4. The following exercises can help the brain reorganize and change itself in a positive way.

    Rituals help to let go of mistaken beliefs:

    The Logical Brain makes changes and adjustments through logic and reason. The Sensory Brain makes changes through dreams, creativity (art, photography, stories, etc.), and rituals. This is why we have events such as weddings, funerals, christenings, etc.

Step 1:

- Take a large piece of paper and write out, in large letters, your beliefs about yourself (i.e. I do not matter/I do not count/Others are more important than me/I am not smart enough).

- Date it and sign it.

- Check in with yourself and see if you are truly ready to let these beliefs go.

- If you are not ready to let go, it's okay. Just keep doing what you're doing, only mindfully.

- If you are ready to let go, rip the paper up/destroy it (burn it, bury it, flush it). Put the shreds of paper into a bag. These beliefs are not true and never were true. You were not born doing this; you developed them because of your experiences.

- As you do the ritual, imagine shedding/letting go of the old beliefs you have carried for so long.

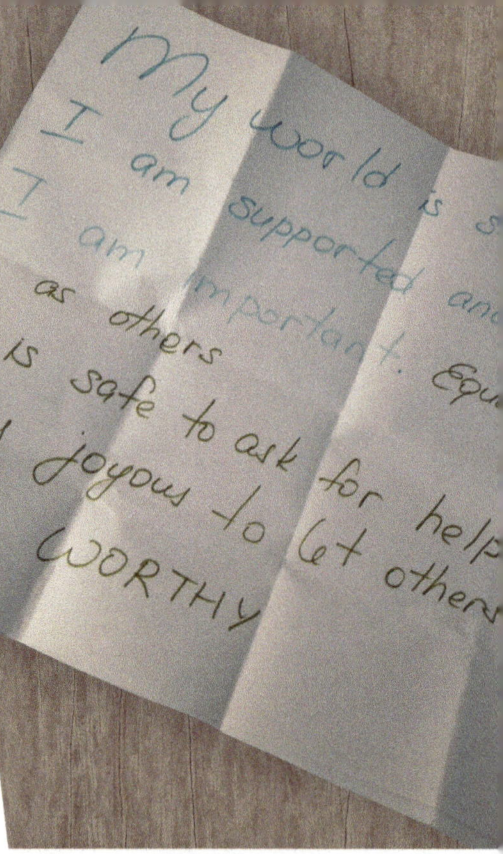

My world is s...
I am supported an...
I am important. Equ...
as others
It is safe to ask for help...
is joyous to let others...
m WORTHY

Step 2:

- Take a large piece of paper.

- Look at the blankness of the paper.

- Write down what you want to believe. You are now choosing what you want to believe. (It will be a living belief, that is, it is true for today, but it could change as you change and your circumstances change).

- Write short statements in the present tense. (i.e. I matter too). If you do not believe that at this moment, then write: I am beginning to believe that I matter too.

- When you have written your new beliefs down, date and sign the piece of paper. (NOTE: If you want to change/edit the piece of paper the next day, do so. It is yours.)

- Fold the paper and keep it. You do not have to read it or look at it. I suggest to clients that they put it in their underwear drawer so that they can see it every day when they get dressed. Or, put it under their pillow and every time the paper crinkles and makes noise, they know what it is a reminder of.

How to Help Others Help Themselves

When someone wants to change how they treat themselves, focus on the positive.

Help the person:

- Identify the behaviour they want to change: i.e., disparaging self-talk (I am no good, I am useless, I suck at this, I am stupid, etc.).

- Brainstorm new behaviours to use instead: i.e., I am okay, I am just learning to do this, I am getting better at this.

- Catch them doing the new behaviours, acknowledge them but do not make a big deal out of it (Hey, you did it! Good going! I like hearing you say that! High 5!)

Key Takeaways:

- You can change your relationship with yourself.

- When you treat yourself badly, your self-esteem goes down; when you treat yourself well, your self-esteem goes up.

- How you treat yourself is a set of habits; habits can be changed.

CHAPTER TEN

Realize and Actualize

*"The butterfly cannot go back
and be the caterpillar."* —Bea Mackay

You have arrived. The previous chapters are all about getting you here.

You did not need to learn anything new. Babies are born knowing how to *process* emotions. Growing up, we learn to *manage* our emotions, which is good in the short term. However, *managing* emotions in the long term is not emotionally or physically healthy. Yoga and meditation are emotionally healthy to do but are not necessary for *processing* emotions.

You need to re-learn to breathe fully and deeply. You need to re-learn to pay attention to the sensations in your body and breathe through the waves of sensations as they get smaller. When you do that, the logical and sensory data are synthesized, creating new neural pathways.

The logical data is from your mind, and the sensory data is from your mind/body—not anyone else's. You can help yourself by learning new information, but ultimately, your mind, thoughts, sensations, and feelings create the new neural pathways.

What Does It Mean to Realize? To Actualize?

To realize is to "wake up" and see people, situations, and circum-stances in a new way—to know in a new way. It is like being underwater and coming to the surface and seeing everything clearly for the first time. It is like being lost in a forest, getting picked up by a hot air balloon, seeing below where you were, and then being put back down again. You cannot un-see what you have seen.

*We tend to make happen
that which we imagine!*

"I used to walk past the White House, and my heart would beat a little faster
as the thought came to me that possibly, possibly I would someday occupy it as
president." —Theodore Roosevelt

To "wake up" is to experience insight, which comes from developing new neural pathways—pathways you did not have before. With insight, decisions precipitate, creating solutions that "Let Things Fall Together." When you synthesize Logical Brain thinking and Sensory Brain sensing, you feel different with new/different/sensations that are pleasant, calm healing and emotionally growthful. You are wiser and more knowledgeable.

A simple example is a toddler learning what "hot" means. He reaches for his mom's cup of hot coffee. She says sharply, "No! Hot!" The toddler touches the cup and quickly pulls his hand away, crying. Now, the word "hot" and the "sensations" of hot are linked. He knows what the word "hot" means and how "hot" feels. The two ways of knowing are integrated.

It is the same with emotions. We can know what depression means, but if we have not experienced depression, we do not know the sensations/feelings. We can know what "in love" means, but if we have never been "in love," we do not know how it feels.

Once you have re-learned how to process your emotions, the choice is yours; you can actualize as little or as much as you choose. Actualizing is about blooming into all that you are genetically capable of becoming. There is no right or wrong. If you have the skills to be an architect but are not interested in the field, be true to yourself. If you want to work in the helping profession, help as much or as little as it suits you. Be true to yourself.

Be True to Yourself

JJ came to see me for help with his vocation. He was a dentist but hated dentistry. His father wanted him to be a dentist, so he went to university and received his degree. His father was very proud of his son. JJ was practising full-time in a dentist's practice. He said he was good at it, it paid well, but he still didn't like it. What he loved doing was playing the saxophone. His hobby was playing free gigs on the weekend, and he wanted to become a full-time musician. He was extremely conflicted about continuing as a dentist.

I worked with him to process his emotions and realign his personal energy. He was battling himself. He had invested many years and a lot of money into becoming a dentist. He enjoyed the respect he got as a dentist. He also didn't want to disappoint his father. However, he was miserable.

At the end of therapy, he was processing his feelings well. He resolved his inner conflict. He decided to work only two days per week as a dentist, and he devoted the rest of his time to his music. He found that he didn't hate dentistry as much once he was actualizing himself as a musician. In fact, he started to enjoy it since it allowed him financially to be a serious musician.

While change is difficult, it is never too late.

No Longer A Cranky Old Woman

My oldest client, Margarita, was 82 when she started therapy. She lived alone. Her second husband of 30 years was in a care home because she could no longer care for him. She visited him almost every day. Her husband had two sons from his previous marriage. She was always arguing with them about their father's care. She had an adult daughter of her own and longed for more contact with her. She constantly reached out to her through emails and the telephone but received little response.

Her health was fragile. Usually, she had two to three appointments per week, and she would usually take a taxi because she was no longer able to drive. Ordering taxis and waiting for them was often a hassle.

She struggled to look after her large home. She couldn't do it herself, so she had to coordinate people to come and do it for her—cleaners, gardeners, handymen, etc.

She wanted her daughter to help her manage her situation, but her daughter had no interest in doing so.

Margarita often called city hall to complain about infractions of the city bylaws, such as someone not picking up after their dog, the workmen working on the property next door using her garbage bins for their refuge, the neighbours walking on her grass, etc. It was no surprise that she was having trouble registering her complaints, so she was also fighting with the city hall clerks. She was worn out from fighting with people.

During therapy, we found that she had unhealed trauma from around the ages of five to seven. This is the age when children often realize they can control things by following the rules and getting others to follow the rules. She had trauma around her father and his abandonment of her at the age of six. She had issues with her mother, who had poor boundaries and couldn't hold her own with her husband. She was traumatized by witnessing the interactions between her parents.

In effect, she was emotionally developmentally arrested around the age of six and perhaps younger. She had been managing her emotions all these years. She was unconsciously recreating the trauma in every aspect of her life.

The therapy consisted of helping her access and express her emotions. We targeted memories related to this time, reliving them, accessing the unhealed emotions, and processing them. I helped her integrate her current-age self with her emotionally young self. In this way, she managed to reclaim her younger age self, who had been frozen in time. That part of her started getting emotionally older.

Margarita said, "I know that old part of me is still there, but I can see beyond it now. I never could see beyond it before." She mostly stopped fighting with others. She commented, "Now I pick my battles." Her relationship with her daughter improved, and they spent more time together. Furthermore, her relationship with others improved significantly. She was no longer "the cranky old lady." She experienced more peace and calmness.

She was 84 when she ended therapy.

Reclaiming Emotionally Hijacked Lives

In this book, there are many examples of reclaimed lives that have been emotionally hijacked by unhealed trauma from the past.

Example 1:

Horatio, who hated his job. One day, he could not put on the "monkey suit" anymore and had been off work ever since, diagnosed with depression. Once he accessed and expressed his repressed rage, his depression lifted, and within weeks, he had found new employment that suited him (see Chapter 7).

Example 2:

The ongoing focus that Sam's parents had on his physical clumsiness created continuing trauma for him. Once he let go of his mistaken belief that he was clumsy, he became adept in every area of his life—sports, business, and leadership (see Chapter 8).

Bea is grateful for the following:

There are so many things in my life for which I am grateful.*

I am most grateful for going through the emotional healing of therapy in my thirties.

Since I was eight years old, my mission in life has been to help others in a significant way.

I am having so much fun and getting satisfaction and fulfillment from achieving my mission.

*Thanks are always appreciated, but what **makes my heart sing** is hearing how people's lives have positively changed from working together.*

*For a complete list, go to beainbalance.com/bea-is-grateful on my website.

Example 3:

Nathalie, who wanted children but was trapped in a 10-year affair. In therapy, she uncovered a trauma she experienced at the age of three when she witnessed the pain on her father's face at her brother's funeral. Somehow, at the age of three, she decided never to have children because it would be too painful to lose them. Once she healed from that buried memory, she ended the affair and started her family with her husband (see Chapter 8).

Example 4:

Lillian, a lonely widow in her mid-50s, who was scaring herself to death every day because she believed she was dying of some illness or disease. In therapy, she changed her relationship with herself by taking responsibility for scaring herself. She interrupted her inner critic and put new kinder behaviours in place. Her energy realigned, and she found a community of people to relate to and joined a church choir (see Chapter 9).

When we let things fall together, magic happens.

—Tereza

Often, I receive thank you notes and cards from clients during and after therapy. These are not testimonials but unsolicited expressions of gratitude for our *process* together.

Example 1:

"In looking back, I remember how 'alive' I felt when I was coming to see Bea. What a great and wonderful influence she had (and still has) on my life! In my own world, I seem to be very helpful to grieving or suffering friends. Perhaps I am paying it (what she gave to me) forward!"

Example 2:

"The work that Bea and I did together was one of the most intense experiences of my life. At that first appointment, I certainly had no idea about the journey I was embarking upon. When therapy ended, I replayed the sessions over and over and wondered if I would ever stop processing them. I'm amazed by how much I have changed over time and in much deeper ways than I could have anticipated. Intriguingly, many of the changes have been so subtle and organic that they slipped beneath my radar until taking the time now to review what has been happening with me. At this point, my past doesn't seem so important. I am sure age has something to do with that, as life is much too short and precious to be stuck somewhere I don't want to be. But I don't think everything can be attributed to my birth date. Something else did happen to me; it is as though the experience in therapy was the point of embarkation for a trip that still is not over, even though at times I have hardly realized that I was still travelling. I always thought I knew where I wanted to go, but it seems I have arrived at various destinations that I couldn't have imagined but that has turned out, almost magically, to be exactly right for me at the moment.

There were, and continue to be the moments of exhilaration that accompany ongoing self-discovery and change. When I look back at it all, I marvel at the

**Write about what you
are grateful for.**

intensity of the work we did together and the years travelled by two people sitting (or not), facing each other (or not) within the confines of one small room!

There are times when it is still challenging to balance the miracle of my reclaimed life now, just as I am—an ordinary woman it turns out, and not the freak of nature I believed I was—and what went before, but even that gets easier."

Example 3:

"I met Bea at a very auspicious time in my life when I didn't have much hope for the future. I was stuck in a horrible relationship with myself, trapped in a marriage where I felt terribly alone, and I was in a career I despised. I was numb, barely clinging to a feeling of aliveness.

I wouldn't exist as the man, husband, and father I am today without having met and worked with Bea. Her voice alone allowed me to be exactly as I was. As she listened and guided me, I gained the confidence to see what demons were holding me back in my life. Working with Bea gave me my life back."

Example 4:

"I was extremely unhappy with my job when I went to see Bea. I felt overworked and underappreciated, but I was afraid to quit. I was conflicted. Instead of talking to me about my indecision, Bea placed two chairs facing each other in the middle of the room and told me to interact with the two sides of myself. She facilitated the interaction. I realized that my inner critic had a lot of power over me, but confronting it helped make my decision clear. It was a powerful exercise. The next day, I quit my job, and the following week, I received an offer from a company I had wanted to work with for years! Without Bea's help, I would have most likely stayed at my old job, feeling miserable and overlooked. Now, whenever I find myself conflicted, I act out the two parts of myself in the comfort of my own home and resolve my issues quicker than ever before. Thanks, Bea!"

Exercise

Develop more neural pathways for the new way of being.

For example:

- Spend time with yourself in the Sensory Brain—use your "senses" to take more of the world in more often.

- Visualize your dreams—imagine "arriving," that is, it has happened already, so enjoy your new way of being.

- Write in a spontaneous and free-flowing style.

- Play more.

How to Help Others Help Themselves

Model for your children how to *process* the sensations of emotions. Modelling is the most powerful way to influence others (friends, students, neighbours, relatives, etc.).

Key Takeaways:

- *Processing* the sensations of emotions helps you become more of who you are.

- Connect with yourself, feel fully alive, and engage in life.

- Live in the moment, be creative and spontaneous.

- Handle current emotional pain and heal from past traumas.

- Experience more peace, joy, and laughter.

- Connect with others in satisfying ways.

About the Author

Dr. Bea Mackay has been helping people reclaim their lives through individual, couples, and family therapy for over 30 years. She offers her clients the missing link to freedom—teaching them how to shift from managing their emotions to processing them. Her book, *The Power of Connection: How to Process Emotion in Turbulent Times* (2020), the companion book to *Let Go of the Outcome and Let Things Fall Together*, focuses primarily on helping people deal with their emotions during turbulent times, specifically during the COVID-19 pandemic. It has been called "a user's guide to the human experience" by Charlie Bowman, president of the Indianapolis Gestalt Institute, and "an owner's manual to help the reader better understand the mysterious and essential part of our being that is our emotional life" by Lindsay Stewart, social worker. Dr. Mackay is also the author of the therapist training manual, *Two-You Work: How to Work with the Self in Conflict* (2011). It has been called a "monumental achievement" and a "fine contribution to counselling and psychology literature" by Ansel Woldt, Emeritus Professor, Kent State University, and the founding member of the Association for the Advancement of Gestalt Therapy. Dr. Mackay is also a senior trainer with Gestalt Vancouver, and she facilitates workshops and lectures at conferences, top universities, and training centers in Canada, the USA, Europe, and Australia. She currently lives in Vancouver, British Columbia, where she enjoys hiking, biking, swimming, walking, and spending time with her son and his family.

Ingram Content Group UK Ltd.
Milton Keynes UK
UKHW050706050623
422881UK00010B/182